John Lyons' The Making of a Perfect Horse

Perfect Horsekeeping
Expert Advice on

Tack and Barn

ISBN: 1-879-620-62-6

Belvoir Publications Inc.
Box 2626
75 Holly Hill Lane
Greenwich, CT 06836 USA

Lyons, John
Perfect Horsekeeping: Expert Advice on Tack and Barn
Lyons, John
and the editors of John Lyons' Perfect Horse

ISBN: 1-879-620-62-6
1. Horses - Training   2. Horsemanship   3. Horses

Manufactured in the United States of America

John Lyons' The Making of a Perfect Horse

Perfect Horsekeeping Expert Advice on

Tack and Barn

John Lyons
and the editors of John Lyons' Perfect Horse

Belvoir Publications, Inc.
Greenwich, CT

Contents

Section II: Expert Advice About Tack

Preface

When we set out to build a house for ourselves, we can approach it either like we're building a temporary chicken coop in the backyard or like we're building a mansion. The difference isn't in the number of rooms — it's in the thoughtfulness that goes into the layout and construction. So, too, the living quarters for our horses can be thrown-together affairs or buildings that are safe, well-ventilated and comfortable.

The *Perfect Horse* writers have interviewed lots of experts — professionals who are tops in their fields — in order to bring you this book. But they've also interviewed lots of everyday horseowners, and we consider their experience as expert advice, too.

We want this book to be a guide as you make decisions about what kind of fencing is most appropriate for your operation, how to string electric wire and what products work best for disinfecting the barn. We want it to teach you how to measure your horse so his saddle fits comfortably, and to know what to look for when you have a trailer hitch installed. But as important as the facts and how-to are, we also want to teach you to think through the many horsekeeping decisions we all have to make. Not all of them involve big expenses. Some are little things, like leaving the barn door open or not, separating new horses or putting them in the same field, or even whether a fan in the barn will help the air flow. That kind of attention to detail can make even a "backyard" barn feel like a mansion — for your perfect horse.

John Lyons

Jesus said, "Do not let your hearts be troubled. Trust in God; trust also in me. In my Father's house are many mansions... And I am going there to prepare a place for you." John 14: 1,2

Section I

Expert Advice
About
The Barn

1

Bringing Horses Home

Making the transition from boarding to keeping horses at home is a larger step than simply buying a place where horses can live in the backyard.

Horse owners long to move to the country for many reasons — to have more horses than they can afford to board at a public facility or to spend more quality time with their equine friends. Some just can't find public facilities to care for their mares and foals. Stallion owners often want their own farm because of the difficulty in boarding stallions, especially when trying to stand a stallion at stud. Bottom line: Horse owners feel that they can provide their horses with better, more specialized care, and they can do it more enjoyably and perhaps for less money than when boarding. But experience doesn't match expectation without realistic planning. **Keeping horses at home can represent a major lifestyle change.**

Before you buy a country home

Research the area before buying a property. Make sure that zoning and the neighbors' attitudes will allow you to have the kind of facility you want. If you are planning to start out with a rural look and add a covered arena later, can you do that? Will flies, dust or a loose horse create a major crisis? And how many horses can you realistically keep on the place?

Obviously, the number of horses you expect to keep will determine how much land you will need. The rule of thumb for most

Keeping a horse at home may mean using a makeshift ring instead of a fenced, level arena. While it may be difficult at first, you'll become a better rider and the horse more responsive when you learn to ignore many distractions and when the horse learns to rely on you instead of the ring fence for direction.

grass-growing areas of the country is two acres of pasture per horse, not only to prevent overgrazing and fighting, but to prevent the horses from trampling the grass to the point that they destroy the root system. When that happens, the pasture becomes a dirt lot.

If you plan to keep your horses stalled much of the time, you may be able to manage with less acreage; however, that means that the property must have a barn or at least corrals. If you plan to leave the horses in the pasture or on dry lot, you'll still need a run-in shed to provide shelter from rain, hot summer sun and cold winter winds. Trees are a great source of shade but do not provide horses adequate shelter from rain, wind and biting flies.

Most horses kept in open pastures still require at least daily feeding. Few suburban pastures are large enough or of high enough quality to allow horses to stay healthy without supplemental feeding. This means that you will need a place to feed the horses and, possibly, some way to separate the horses while they eat. After feeding, they can be released back into the pasture.

Whether your horses are stabled or pastured, the property will probably need at least one large shed for storing hay. It is not safe to store hay in the barn where the horses are kept. Hay sheds should be at least 50 feet from any other structure and should be well-ventilated to prevent heat buildup.

Fencing is another major consideration. The most important fence is the perimeter one, since it keeps the horses on your property. It should be well constructed of safe materials. Barbed wire and square hog wire should be avoided, as they can easily injure horses. Cross fencing is desirable to divide the pastures into smaller sections. Ideally, a property will be divided into at least two sections so that horses can be rotated from one pasture to another. This prevents overgrazing and allows the grass to reestablish itself. If your horses must be kept separate from each other, or if you will be standing a stallion, more cross fencing may be needed to establish several smaller paddocks.

Then, of course, there's the question of where to ride. Open land around you doesn't necessarily translate to land to ride on. Land owners are getting increasingly careful about both liability issues and erosion issues. Building and maintaining an arena is a bigger (and more ongoing) project than most people realize.

Lifestyle considerations

Family commitment: Working together on the farm can provide a focal point for family activities. There are so many chores to be done, everyone must play a part. It will surely reduce the time spent watching television, talking on the phone and surfing the Internet. It is a great opportunity for children to learn to take responsibility. When children participate in the maintenance of the farm, they learn how to tackle problems and devise solutions — it's a great confidence builder. On the other hand, if farm life is only one person's dream, it can cause big family tensions.

Commuting time: It is not uncommon for country or suburban dwellers to have an hour-long commute to the office. When you add two (or more) hours of driving to your daily schedule, this considerably reduces your free time, not to mention the costs of gas and wear and tear on your vehicle. If your current lifestyle involves chauffeuring your children from one activity to another, you may find that these activities become a problem due to the long commute times, and it's harder for kids to maintain old friendships.

Stall cleaning: If you expect to keep your horses stalled, plan on allowing at least 20 minutes per stall to clean a stall that has been occupied by a horse for 12 hours. This doesn't sound significant, unless it's multiplied by four or more horses.

Getting away from home: Don't plan to leave home for any length of time. It is not generally difficult to find someone to care for your pet dog or cat. But finding someone to feed horses twice daily and clean stalls may be considerably more difficult. You must find someone who is competent to care for the horses, knowledgeable enough to know how to handle a horse emergency, and has enough free time that they can do your chores for you.

Property maintenance: Maintaining a country home is labor intensive. We have talked about the daily chore of cleaning stalls, but there are other considerations. Fences need repairs. Pastures must be mowed. Equipment breaks down and must be repaired. Each of these things must be handled, and it is often difficult to hire someone to do these types of chores. And, if you are living on a budget, it can get costly quickly. Before making the choice to live in the country, carefully evaluate your ability (and willingness) to take on these kinds of challenges. But for people who enjoy constantly being busy, it is a wonderful lifestyle. Those people who are more sedentary may be overwhelmed dealing with these country home crises.

No one to ride with: Remember how frustrating it is when a fellow boarder took one of your brushes, or your fly spray disappeared? When you keep horses at home, that won't happen, but you probably won't have anyone to chat with as you groom or to ride out with, either. You won't have someone to watch your horse jog for soundness or fellow boarders to learn from. In fact, keeping your horses at home can be downright lonely and, in some cases, dangerous if you will be riding alone.

Too many horses: You start out with your own two horses, then befriend an old foundered pony who needs a good home. Add to that your best friend's horse, since you don't want to ride alone and it will be nice to have someone to help with chores occasionally. And, who hasn't dreamed of starting a young horse? With the cost of weanlings so much less than grown horses, a weanling is a must-have. But he can't grow up alone, so two weanlings arrive instead of one. Now, your spouse or kids are interested in the occasional trail ride, but alas, none of the horses you already have are suitable, so add one old reliable trail horse, and on it goes. Suddenly the feed bill and the chores both skyrocket, and your riding time evaporates.

And now, instead of leading horses around, improving their halter manners at the same time, you herd them from place to place. Suddenly, sweet horses become herd-oriented, and family members complain that their horses are hard to catch, or worse yet, lay their ears back at feeding time. Your horse isn't safe to ride on the trail because he's obsessed with getting back to his buddies, and your lifestyle choice has become a bad dream, as you fight feelings of frustration and fatigue and wish for the old days when you drove to the boarding barn, carrots in tow. You rode your horse and then drove away, leaving the headaches behind.

A day in the life

The alarm goes off at 4:30 a.m. You drag yourself out of bed, pulling on your barn clothes as you go. In the barn, eight hungry horses impatiently wait for breakfast. You measure out everyone's portion, adding supplements as needed. As you feed each horse, you check that he has no injuries and still has his shoes on.

After everyone has been fed, you rinse and refill 16 water buckets. A quick trip out to the pasture shows that the water trough needs to be filled, too. Back in the barn, you clean stalls while you wait for the horses to finish eating. When everyone is finished with breakfast, you turn each horse into the pasture. You haven't finished cleaning the stalls, but it is 6, time to get ready for work. By 7, you have transformed yourself into a business professional and are on your way to the office. If there are no major problems on the interstate, you will be at work by 8.

Things are busy at the office, with more to do than three people could accomplish. Finally, at 6 p.m., you decide that everything not done today must wait until tomorrow. The drive home isn't too bad, since you have worked through the worst of the rush-hour traffic, and by 7, you are home. You go inside, check your phone messages and get into your barn clothes.

Outside, you call the horses up from the pasture and get everyone settled in their stalls, once again checking for injury, lameness or lost shoes. Once again, you measure out the feed, distribute dinner and top off the water buckets. While the horses eat, you finish cleaning the stalls that you didn't have time to clean that morning. By 8:30, you are finished in the barn and are more than ready for your own supper. At 10:30, you call it a day and head off to bed, dreaming of the weekend, when you'll have a chance to ride the horses. In the midst of your beautiful dream, you remember that the pastures are ready for mowing, the stalls must be stripped, all those fences need to be sprayed with herbicide. And then there's cooking dinner for the family. Ah, yes, the family ...

Enjoying life in the country

Now that we've raised lots of possible negatives, the above scenario doesn't have to be your reality. The key is being proactive — planning, rather than just having to react as each matter presents itself. Talk with lots of folks who own their own farm and try to match their answers with what you see. If they tell you their farm doesn't take much time to maintain, do you want yours to look like theirs? If so, what conveniences have they installed?

Decide what your budget really is, then pad it for the unexpected. Decide how many horses you can realistically enjoy, and what you'll do during soccer season when the kids aren't available to help with chores. How will you manage if you get the flu — can someone cover for you?

Decide if you are planning to take in boarders, and if so, under what arrangement. Talk with your insurance company about such things as your coverage if friends come to ride and are injured. Having worked out all the above, turn your attention to enjoying the choices you've made.

Prioritize pleasure time: When you have land, horses and a house to maintain, there will always be chores. The endless list of "things to do" is normal. Many people make the mistake of thinking that they are not allowed to ride or enjoy themselves until all the chores are done. This is the first step to disillusionment. When making that to-do list for the upcoming weekend, riding your horse should be a top priority. Try riding first thing in the morning, before beginning your weekend chores. If you don't, you may find the day gone.

Enjoy your chores: Chores aren't bad — they are a lifestyle — and most folks enjoy them once they get into a routine. It may sound absurd to tell someone to enjoy cleaning stalls and washing water buckets, but the reality is that you will spend a lot of time performing these tasks. In actuality, barn chores can be a relaxing break from an otherwise hectic day. It is quiet in the barn, and the sound of horses munching their hay can be soothing. As you clean each stall, take time to give some attention to the horse in the stall. Rub his

There are few things as rewarding as seeing your children, dogs and horses all enjoying a life together.

head and scratch his special itchy spot. Giving your horse some attention is good for him and will make you feel better, too.

Make use of available services: You will quickly discover that time becomes a precious commodity. Make the most of any service that you can afford, especially for repetitive tasks. If you can afford to pay someone to do barn work or mowing, this will allow you the freedom to enjoy your horses. When purchasing feed, hay and stall bedding, consider buying it from suppliers who will deliver their products and stack them in your barn. It may cost a little more, but the extra cash outlay may be worth it.

Acquire the equipment: Plan to buy equipment, and then more equipment, in addition, of course, to your trailer-pulling truck and your farm truck (which allows you to save wear and tear on your good truck). Then you may find yourself buying a commuter car to save on gas.

Property maintenance will be simplified if you have the right equipment for the job. The size tractor you'll need depends upon the number of acres you have and the size of the brush mower you will be pulling. The size of the brush mower will depend upon the size of your paddocks. If you opt for a large mower, you may also find that you require a small one for getting into tight spaces. And you can be sure that there will be areas where mowing with the tractor is not feasible. A hand-held weed eater may be necessary for trimming around buildings and fences. You may also want to buy one of the walk-behind-type trimmer/mowers. They are much easier to use when large stretches of trimming are required.

Many people find that, although their time for riding is limited, doing chores, enjoying nature and getting exercise can be fun.

Mowing around fences is always a problem. The best solution is to keep the fence lines sprayed with herbicide to discourage grass from growing under the fence. You may need to buy a large tank sprayer to apply the herbicide. If you have a concrete aisle in the barn, you will find that a leaf blower is a great way to keep the barn aisle swept. If you are keeping four or more horses in a barn, a manure spreader is invaluable for disposing of manure and providing organic fertilizer to your pastures at the same time (with, of course, a tractor, an all-terrain vehicle or a large riding lawn mower to pull the manure spreader).

Expectations vs. reality

Expectation: When horse owners dream of living in the country, they assume they will have more time to devote to the horses — after all, the horses are so convenient. No need to waste time driving across town to the stable. Just step out of the house, and there they are!

Reality: Expectation becomes reality for school-aged children. They are able to spend time with their horses every day after school and during summer vacations, without needing a parent to take them to the stable. But it is less true for adults. For adults who work in the city, a commute to and from the farm/home may be added to the work day, making it even more difficult to find time for the horses. Add the amount of time required to maintain the property, and many country dwellers find themselves spending those precious summer weekends riding a tractor instead of their horses.

Expectation: Horse owners envision reducing the cost of owning horses, since the cost of hay, feed and bedding will probably be less than monthly boarding fees and since they can do the work themselves.

Reality: This works only in the strictest sense of actual cash outlay for these things. Total expenses, however, will probably be considerably higher. A rural setting, with a home, farm buildings, acreage and fencing, entails substantial upkeep, requiring both time and money. And then there are a million unanticipated expenses.

Expectation: One of the greatest enticements for living in the country is the ability to provide a customized environment for your horse, without the need to consult with a barn manager or stable owner.

Reality: Reality meets expectation here. When you are in control of the property, you can control all aspects of a horse's life. This is an invaluable asset when raising foals, owning stallions or caring for those old retirees. However, it often also means you are alone.

Life in the country has its own special pleasures that make the hard work all worthwhile. You enjoy the millions of stars on a clear night when you do late night barn checks. You can enjoy glorious sunrises as you feed the horses in the mornings and vivid sunsets as you are again feeding and cleaning up. Wildlife is abundant and visible, with deer grazing in your fields. Rabbits abound and provide food for the hawks and owls that you will often see sitting on power poles and tall trees. If you have a lake or a pond on your property, you may have geese or herons arrive seasonally and raise their young.

With nature so close at hand, you develop an appreciation for its beauty and its natural cycles. There is something calming about the song of the meadowlark that makes stall cleaning a little less tedious. And seeing a deer dart across the pasture certainly enlivens the monotony of mowing pastures. It's all you envisioned and more. It's a big commitment and a lot of work but if the lifestyle fits, you wouldn't trade it for all the world.

Plan your facilities

You want repetitive tasks to be time-efficient. There are things you can have installed on your property to help streamline your work load:

Water faucets: Try to eliminate the use of long water hoses. Dragging hoses out and rewinding them after use takes valuable time. And, in the winter, they are an extra problem, since all water must be removed from them to avoid freezing and damage to the hose.

Locate a water faucet (or automatic waterer, if you can afford it) at every stall or corral. Short washing-machine hoses are a great way to get water from the faucet into the water bucket. If you live in cold climates, consult with a plumber about ways to insulate the faucets to avoid freezing. Many people install the plumbing in such a manner that there is a valve that allows the water to be drained from the pipes in severe weather.

If you have water troughs in your pastures, install frost-free water faucets at each trough. This allows you to easily refill the tanks without the need to drag hoses from another location. In mild weather, you can install a short hose and a tank float that will automatically keep the tank full. These may have to be removed in winter to prevent water in the faucet from freezing, however.

Stall mats: If you keep horses in stalls on a regular basis, rubber stall mats are an amazing time saver. They make the stalls easier to clean, and they protect the base of the stall floor. Without mats, the stall floors will develop holes in the areas where the horses urinate. Over time, as you dig out the wet spots, the stall floor will become pitted. It will be necessary to re-level the floor by adding dirt or gravel. Rubber mats also reduce the amount of bedding required, since they provide a cushion for the horse's legs. Stall mats are big-ticket items and installing them is a major effort, but they'll save you both money and time in the long run.

Electric fences: No matter what type of fence you have, maintenance will be considerably reduced with the use of a "hot wire." Horses love to chew on board fences. They will push against mesh fencing, causing it to stretch and loosen its attachment to the posts. Straight-wire fencing suffers when the horses reach through it to graze on the other side. Run an electric wire around the inside of all board and mesh fences. Electrify multiple strands of straight wire fences. You will see a significant decrease in the amount of repair work required to keep your fences maintained. PH

2

Buying Horse Property

What to watch for and what to watch out for —
that's what we wanted to know from realtor
Madelon Wallace regarding purchasing a horse farm.

Horse-farm ownership is a dream become a reality, not just for life-long horsemen but for people from all walks of life. Often, new farm owners have a knowledge of their own sport, but not much experience in keeping horses or managing a farm. Madelon Wallace's equine experience spans the gamut from foxhunting to showing to managing training facilities and horse shows. Concerned about seeing the land she loves broken up indiscriminately and property buyers making decisions that end up costing them dearly, she entered the real estate market and specializes in horse properties. We asked her to give us advice about buying horse property, especially for the first-farm buyer.

Perfect Horse: *What's the first advice you give to someone planning to buy a horse property?*

Wallace: The land is usually the least expensive part of the whole endeavor. Don't skimp on the land, either the quality or the quantity. You can always change the house or build another barn, but you can't change the land or the location.

PH: *How does a buyer end up with too little land?*

Wallace: Often first-time buyers have unrealistic ideas about how much land they need for a satisfactory arrangement. They buy five

Madelon Wallace discusses important land-use issues with a future champion.

acres, and by the time they've built a house and barn, a driveway, fencing and a riding area — and have added several extra horses — they feel crowded.

Your needs will depend on the type of operation you have. If you have grass pastures and plan to keep your horses out on grass most of the time, you'll want enough land to allow for good grazing and pasture rotation. If the horse-to-grass ratio is too low, you won't be able to maintain the pastures — you just can't get the growth of grass. Your property will look like a mud hole.

If you have enough land and can grow good grass, you'll have fewer parasite problems, the property will look better, your horses will stay cleaner and your feed costs will be lower. Additionally, acreage always provides a buffer between your horses and the neighbors.

PH: *Assuming most of your clients have a budget, what do you mean about skimping on quality?*

Wallace: Any way you look at it, a cheap, poor piece of land will cost more to maintain and to develop than good-lying land. Often, people are determined not to pay over "x" dollars per acre for their land, so they end up buying land that will cost them lots more in improvements than if they paid two or more times "x" per acre. Clearing and grading is expensive, and often you end up with drainage or other on-going problems.

You have to evaluate what concessions you really can make. If you have pleasure horses, perhaps a big hill or wooded pasture is suitable, but foals need pastures that are relatively free of places they can get into trouble. If you live at the top of a long, steep driveway, you have to be sure the feed truck and farrier can make it up the hill in the winter.

A property with water on it, a good flowing stream, is ideal, if you can afford it. A stream usually makes a property worth more. (But due to concerns about EPM and other organisms, and erosion, you may end up fencing the horses out of the stream.) A small slow-flowing stream can turn into a mudhole after the horses dig and play in it. Lowland, or bottom land, is usually less expensive because it can't be built on, but it can make great pasture because it will hold moisture. When it floods, you'll have to make some other arrangements for your horses.

Then, look at the other amenities and natural advantages. Trees provide an airy shade that is cooler for the horses than standing in a run-in shed. A sand lot for turnout in wet weather will prevent your pastures from being torn up. Using it for turnout in the spring will give your pastures a chance to get a good growth of grass before they are eaten down. If your property is on a hill, you are going to have erosion problems or will incur a cost to prevent them. If the hill is in a pasture, your horses are going to tear it up. People forget that a horse is a big animal, and hooves create big divits.

Whatever you do, don't buy mediocre land just because you like the house. You can build a house anywhere, but you are stuck with the land and the location. Just because the previous owner put a fence up and labeled it "horse property," doesn't mean it's land you'd choose for a horse farm or training operation.

Your need for land — for pasture, arenas or trail riding — may vary greatly from one part of the country to another.

PH: *What should a buyer consider about pasture?*

Wallace: Just as you have to mow a lawn, you have to maintain a field. A property that works for you and looks decent takes work. If your pastures are broken into fields too small, you'll have to muck them out, which is time- and labor-intensive.

The more nutritious the grass, the better off your horses will be and the lower your feed bills. Animals do reflect the property they graze. Obviously, the first consideration about the pasture is the soil. If the soil is sandy, the footing is great, but it's hard to grow grass and you often encounter sand-colic problems. If it's rocky, it won't grow grass well, and you may have to live with the occasional stone bruise. If the soil is wet, you'll need to be concerned about keeping the right moisture in your horse's feet and not losing shoes.

Agricultural extension agents can be of tremendous help. They'll tell you what grasses grow best in your area and what intervals to water, bushhog or mow.

PH: *What else should a buyer take into account?*

Wallace: What are your expectations? Who is going to do the work? How much are you willing to mow? Are you realistic about the

Lowland or bottom land, if it drains well, can make excellent pasture. But if it's too sandy, it's hard to get a good growth of grass.

availability of reliable help in the area? First-time property buyers have a hard time visualizing how much time and money it takes to keep a property up. Everything about it takes work, and no one is getting any younger. People have to ask themselves not just if this will be fun for now, but can they maintain it as they get older. Of course, a lot has to do with the condition of the farm and how well it is laid out.

Layout plays a huge factor in convenience. For instance, if your pastures have shade, that saves bedding and stall cleaning because you may then be able to keep your horses outside in the heat of the day. If your barn is wide enough to drive through, you may save yourself wheelbarrow time.

Occasionally, I find the main reason people want a property is they think keeping a horse at home will be cheaper than boarding. If finances are the only consideration, they'll probably be better off at a boarding facility than taking on the expense, responsibility and work of a property.

Socializing is important. People often think how wonderful it will be just to walk outside and ride any time they want. But they often find either they don't have time to ride because of the amount of work, or they don't want to ride alone. While there may be a certain status in having your own place, people with their own farm sometimes find they miss riding with friends. There's no one to help keep them motivated, no shared goals, no one to watch how a horse is moving if you think he's off. But then, on the other hand, there's no one to "borrow" your brushes or tack.

All that said, there are few things as satisfying as watching your horses out the kitchen window or a late-night check of the barn and having your horse nicker to you.

PH: *We've heard the maxim that there are three things important in real estate: location, location and location. Does this apply when establishing a horse farm?*

Wallace: It's extremely important. The first consideration for most horse people is where to ride. Although property on a trail system or with trail access is more expensive, it is usually well worth the difference in money. If you have to hook up a trailer each time you want to ride, it probably isn't going to happen. And, the extra money you'll pay to live in an area where you can ride the trails generally isn't as much as the cost of building and maintaining a ring. And access to trails greatly affects resale value — especially as communities grow and horse people find themselves without places to ride.

Many times it looks like there is plenty of room to ride, but when you actually go out, you find yourself locked out. You may be surrounded by 600 beautiful acres, but if you don't have permission to ride there, you are back to trotting around on your own five acres. Beyond trail riding, if the owner has interest in breeding, boarding or running a training barn, then some areas are suitable and others not.

PH: *What should a buyer look for in a realtor?*

Wallace: Choose your realtor carefully. I would definitely do some research before I got connected with a real estate agent — don't just get a friend of a friend to help you. This is one area where it's important to know both the land and the needs of your operation. Just because someone isn't a horse person doesn't mean they aren't a good realtor, but if they aren't familiar with horse operations like yours, you'd better know specifically what your needs are. A knowledgeable realtor can help you find your way around the local horse community.

Once you've moved

Once you've moved, be a good neighbor. Not everyone loves horses, but many accept the fact that a well-kept place helps the community retain charm or a rural feeling. Don't take liberties with someone else's property, riding on it without permission, riding across fields instead of on the edge of the field, or riding through orchards or groves and inadvertently breaking sprinkler pipes as you go. Riding on someone else's land is a privilege, not a right. Get involved in the community and let your horses add value.

PH: *What are the major concerns as to choice of community?*

Wallace: You have to determine what is most important to you. Land and lifestyle are connected. It's getting more difficult to maintain a ranching or horse-farm lifestyle. You have to be in an area where the neighbors are like-minded, where horse property is seen as adding value to the community.

Don't just fly in, find a place you love and buy it. Get to know some of the horse people before you move. Some communities are friendly and don't care what discipline you ride. Others are more snobbish, and it may be a long time before you fit in. This is especially important if you are relocating a business and will be dependent on local clientele.

Talk with the veterinarians about what services are available in the area. If your operation requires a lot of high-tech diagnostics and plan to live in the boonies, you may be disappointed.

Find out what's going on in the community. Is it horse friendly? Is there a possibility that the zoning is going to change and put you out of business? Is there a restriction on the number of horses you may have (separate from what is good for the horses?), because once you have a farm, you will likely find yourself with more horses than you planned.

PH: *What about once you've located a property?*

Wallace: Walk the land. Ride or drive it, if it's too large to walk. Get to know for yourself what is on the property, where the wet spots are, if you really can see the mountains from the pasture and where the property lines fall. Don't just walk around the homesite or barn area. Make sure you know where you are going to ride. It doesn't do you as much good to be close to a trail system if you have to cross a busy road to get there.

Land with a mountain view, rolling pasture, flat area for an arena and access to a trail system is a lot to ask for.

While it reduces the amount of pasture, putting your fence back from the road is safer for the horses and makes your place look prettier.

Find out what your neighbors are doing — or what they can do. You may build a beautiful farm, only to have some undesirable business move in next to you because the zoning is unrestricted. Find out what the plans are for the county or town, the proposed roads and other major changes.

Be sure about your water supply. Where does your water come from and how much does it cost? Horse operations are water-intensive. Check about taxes. Sometimes living in one place is far less expensive than just over the line into the next county or state.

PH: *What about land-use issues?*

Wallace: Years ago, one could ride all day without a fence, but that's not the case today. Big tracts of land are getting chopped up, although it can be done in ways that preserve the feel of the community and the lay of the land. Once an area gets built up, it won't get unbuilt. You can't enjoy horses without land, and if we aren't good caretakers of the land, we won't have anywhere to ride. Good horse property is getting harder to come by. If we want to continue to enjoy our lifestyle, we have to take responsible care of the land and our community. ■PH■

3

Personal Security
At The Barn

*Knowing what you'll do "if and when"
will allow you to feel confident and not worry.*

When our editorial team first discussed a chapter about staying safe from unwanted visitors to your barn, it seemed far fetched. Like most horsepeople, we feel our barns are a place of refuge from the real world. But, truth is, we often ride and keep our horses in the same area where folks lock their doors both in the daytime and at night. We leave our jobs in the dark of winter and ride, often alone. We go to the barn late at night to check a sick horse, and we travel alone to horse shows.

Are we trying to scare you? No. But you may not be aware of potential security problems at your barn. A little homework goes a long way toward keeping you and your horse safe. Just as we speak of someone as "street smart," aware of the hazards in the big city, we need to become "farm smart." Let's look first at a horse operation from the perspective of someone with a potentially hostile intent.

Trouble may be logical

"If you can afford horses, you must be rich" is a common belief. Never mind what horsepeople often sacrifice for their animals; you may seem to have enough money for barn help, fancy halters and a recent-model vehicle. So someone who wants money, particularly if that person is chemically dependent, may see your farm as a potential source of something to steal.

Closed-circuit television can film everything from what goes on in the barn to the entire indoor arena. The system at this facility plays views from four cameras at once on a TV screen in the office.

People are more transient now than in years past, and, in fact, most people are not long-term residents of the community in which they work. That means we know little about the background of our employees, clients or visitors to the barn. Not only does our country have a homeless population, we have a population of people living in homes they detest or feel unsafe in. It's not unlikely in some areas to find someone in your barn just looking for shelter.

Then there are troublemakers — those same "jerks" who think it's fun to honk horns or harass riders on the road.

And, there are those who don't want you to have what they can't afford. So, angry at their lot in life, they strike out at people who have a lifestyle they envy.

Random violence is real and probably the most difficult crime to deal with. But what about "logical violence" — the client who didn't think he was treated right, or someone's old boyfriend, or a person who's had too much to drink? And most importantly, how can you protect yourself and your horses from those intending to do bodily harm? In addition to recognizing that unwelcome visitors may come onto your property, it's important to differentiate if they pose a threat or not.

If it doesn't feel right

We don't want to be inhospitable — it goes against all our codes of horsemanship, from the cowboy ethic to the fox-hunting tradition. So when our intuition warns us about someone, we tend to dismiss our nagging thought as silly; but we should learn to do otherwise. Our intuition processes information from different sources faster than we can consciously think.

When engrossed in working with our horse or doing chores, we may miss important warning signs. Crime victims frequently report knowing something was wrong, but they ignored the feeling because it didn't seem rational.

You know the normal noises in your barn. If you hear something that doesn't sound right and you are worried about checking it out alone, go for help.

Many crimes, such as rape and assault, are committed by people who are so familiar to us that we assume them to be safe. Be aware of unusual or aggressive behavior. For instance, a person standing too close as he talks to you, and who moves in even after you back up, is showing aggressive behavior.

Plan how you'll respond in a personal emergency. Determine in advance how and where to call for help and what measures you can take until help arrives.

Think through what you'd do if Plan A fails. If you are counting on your dog to protect you and he gets locked in a stall — or worse yet, shot — you are unprotected. If you can't get to the phone or the power is out and your cordless phone doesn't work, what will you do?

Unwelcome visitors

Deterring less-than-friendly visitors from coming onto your farm is a primary defense. The following are worth consideration:

■ Signs indicating that a security system is in effect, that your dogs are not just pets or that visitors are welcome only by appointment.

■ A gate at the end of the driveway means that someone must stop to open it or approach your barn on foot.

■ Good lighting. People with intent to commit a crime do not want to be seen. Install motion sensor lights inside and outside the barn.

■ Be sure that you can see the approach to the barn. That might mean trimming bushes so there is nowhere to hide or parking your trailer in another spot.

Learn to trust your instincts. When checking a suspicious activity, better to have help and stay safe than be alone and risk injury.

■ Ideally, you want to be able to drive all the way around the barn and paddocks, so you can shine headlights to investigate something suspicious.

■ Reduce attractions. Don't leave tack in the aisleways or storage sheds unlocked, or money in the office. Ask boarders to lock their valuables in their trunks and to lock their vehicles.

■ Keep your place tidy. When things are in order and vehicles parked in a line, it's easier to spot something out of place — that visibility issue again.

■ Nothing like yappy dogs or a noisy goose to announce the arrival of company. While the critters may not be great defense, no experienced thief wants his arrival announced.

■ Closed-circuit observation systems are now reasonably priced. Also, readily visible telephones or walkie-talkies convey the impression that there is help nearby.

Personal safety measures

Just as it takes mental discipline to always work with our horses from a position of control — indeed, that's a good part of what the Lyons training is all about — it takes a change in mindset to train ourselves to operate from a position of safety. We don't like to think anything bad will happen, but better to think through your safety routes in advance and ask yourselves what you can do to stay safe.

For instance, let's say you are at home and hear the dogs barking about 10 p.m. at the barn. Should you:

A. Yell at the dogs to be quiet, or

B. Walk down to the barn to investigate, carrying a flashlight, or

C. Drive from the house to the barn with your vehicle doors locked?

To operate from a position of safety, you'd drive to the barn, though it may be a short distance. If it turns out the dogs only found a skunk, you'll be glad to be inside your truck. And, should there be a trespasser, you may be able to see them in your truck lights, chase them off while you are still safely inside the truck or, from the safety of the truck, use your cell phone to call for help. Someone who only intended to steal may become violent when personally confronted. By staying inside the truck, you may prevent personal injury.

Develop routines that put you in advantageous positions. Park your vehicle so you can drive away without backing up.

The buddy system works. Aside from the obvious danger from falling while riding alone, a person alone (particularly a woman) is more approachable and vulnerable than when there are two or three people together.

Do you keep your cell phone accessible? And have you programmed it so you can make an emergency call in a hurry? If so, good. If you are planning to dial 9-1-1 in an emergency, you'd better check that it's available in the area and find out where that call goes. It generally goes to the emergency center nearest the home base of the phone service. So if your phone service is based 40 miles away — or 2,000 miles away — you are not going to get help fast. Better think about using the local seven-digit emergency or police number.

If you are faced with the possibility of personal assault, your first objective is to escape — get away. Is there a safe place you can go? Is there an office or tack room with a lock on the inside, so you can lock yourself in and others out? If the

Dogs and signs are good deterrents for casual opportunists, but don't rely on them against someone with serious criminal intent.

room has an outside window, you want a phone you can dial in the dark. You don't want to be a visible target.

Organize a neighborhood watch system; at least get in the habit of touching base with neighbors and recognizing their vehicles and work schedules. Let someone know your schedule. If you should run into trouble of any kind, hopefully they will come looking for you.

Develop an alert, positive, assertive demeanor, not a passive one. Predators look for easy, unaware targets.

Think about potential "weapons" so you don't have to lose critical time should a crisis arise. Throwing a bucket of washwater or a set of body clippers at someone may buy you time to escape.

Educate yourself about self-protection and staying safe. Learn people skills. Not every stranger on your property is a predator. Understanding dangerous behavior helps keep us from being victimized.

When you have unwanted company

What if, despite precautions, you are faced with a threat of bodily injury? Run. Even if someone is hurting your horse, you can't help the horse if you are injured. Get away and call for help.

Meeting force with force is dangerous; even if you win the struggle, you may be injured. Fighting, particularly with a weapon, is a personal decision that should be thought through before you are in that situation. In most states it is not legal to use deadly force to protect your property.

Don't let the fear of personal assault affect the enjoyment of your horse activities. If you are nervous about being safe, you'll begin short-cutting your visits to the barn. Encountering problems is the exception, not the rule, but taking the right precautions is the smart thing to do. ▣

4

Stable Environments

No matter what your budget,
even a few small barn improvements can add
big benefits to your horse's health and happiness.
A world-renowned barn expert tells you how.

If you're a typical horseperson, you enjoy *barn* cleaning and barn improvements more than *house* cleaning and home improvements. For advice on making barns — both old and new — as horse-hospitable as possible, we turned to Chenault Woodford at CMW, Inc., in Lexington, Ky.

Woodford has been called the "grand maestro of equine architecture," and rightfully so. The architectural planner for the Kentucky Horse Park, his firm also designed such renowned equine facilities as the grandly elegant Gainsborough Farm in Versailles, Ky., and the L'Esprit Arabian horse community in northern Kentucky. He's currently completing designs for the first major Thoroughbred breeding and training facility in Central Asia's Kazakhstan.

To help redesign some features of your barn, Woodford outlines the elements of good barn design, emphasizing that the following priorities and principles are as applicable in backyard barns as they are in multimillion dollar facilities.

Preliminary principles

"In any construction project, but especially in a barn, money spent must yield maximum value," Woodford says. Getting the best return on your investment relates to several factors, including how much time you spend in the barn and with your horse. The most critical consideration, however, is how your horse lives. "The more barn-bound your horse is, the more effort you'll need to make to optimize his well-being," Woodford comments. "Some horses have no turnout time at all. Under poor conditions, keeping a horse in a stall is like putting him in prison, physically and mentally. So, if your horses spend most of their time inside, at least make your barn the best environment you reasonably can afford."

Air quality is priority one

"The top priority in any barn is air quality," Woodford says. "Improving the 'climate' inside is the single best thing you can do to improve the health of barn-bound horses."

Inside a barn, climate control hinges on air movement. Ventilation not only replaces stale air and dissipates odors, it also helps reduce humidity and temperature. High humidity encourages the growth of mold and fungus, which can pose serious respiratory and digestive dangers for horses, as well as blanket your tack with mildew.

Unfortunately, barn humidity can rise quickly. "A thousand-pound horse puts two gallons of moisture into the air every day just by breathing," Woodford points out. "That doesn't count urine or kicked-over water buckets or all the dribbling and drooling a horse does when he eats and drinks."

Ideal humidity is 40 to 60 percent. Of course, in many areas of the country, it's hard to keep even household humidity below 60 percent. "But homes are closed up tighter than barns," Woodford says, "and air movement is key to keeping humidity down."

Temperature is another factor in the climate equation. "The ideal temperature range for a horse is 40 to 70 degrees Fahrenheit," says Woodford. "No matter where you live, you should insulate your barn. In winter, with nominal insulation but no supplemental heat, your barn will stay 15 degrees warmer inside. So, if it's 25 degrees outside, your horse will still be perfectly comfortable, even without a blanket." Insulating the barn's ceiling and perimeter walls will also help reduce humidity by cutting down on inside condensation.

While keeping your horse warm in winter isn't difficult, keeping him cool in summer can be a challenge. "If it's 90 degrees outside, you simply can't cool your barn down to 70 degrees inside without air conditioning. Who can afford that?" Woodford says wryly. "But you can keep your horses more comfortable with plenty of air movement, which helps a sweating horse cool more quickly. The hotter your locale, the more air movement your barn needs."

To boost natural ventilation in a new barn, align its main aisle to catch prevailing summer breezes, which typically blow from west to east. Also, in each stall, install doors or large windows that open to the outside.

"Even in the South, a well-designed barn with lots of natural air flow may not need fans," Woodford notes. "In ill-positioned or poorly designed barns, however, you'll need equipment that moves a hundred cubic feet of fresh air per minute per thousand pounds of animal weight. And that's for temperatures below 60 degrees; you'll need even more when it's warmer. Even with an ideal temperature, you still need plenty of ventilation to take out odors, reduce humidity and replace fresh air."

Safe footing and plenty of light and air go a long way to keeping a horse's attitude cheery.

To reduce humidity in a closed space, such as a feed or tack room, Woodford suggests installing an inexpensive window-unit air conditioner or a dehumidifier. "That's an easy $200 to $250 solution to the problem of mold," he says. "A dehumidifier will actually warm the room somewhat, since the motor discharges heat into the room. So in a northern locale, a dehumidifier may be a good choice, where an air conditioner is a better option for barns in warmer parts of the country."

Next, what's underfoot?

Your second priority should be flooring, particularly in stalls. While a soft place to sleep is helpful, proper drainage is critical, not only for respiratory fitness, but also for hoof health. That's why, whatever flooring you choose, Woodford recommends that you put it over a gravel base, 10 to 12 inches thick, with perforated pipe that drains to the outside. Any urine or water that isn't absorbed by bedding will simply drain off through the gravel.

"I never recommend concrete stall floors, and I don't like dirt either," says Woodford. "Concrete is much too hard on horses' legs, and with urine-soaked dirt, you end up with holes in your floor from mucking out wet spots. If your budget is tight, the lowest-cost flooring that makes any sense at all is a gravel bed topped with a layer of finely crushed stone. That drains pretty well, but it's dusty. So when you can afford it, put rubber mats down on top of that."

In Woodford's opinion, rubber mats over gravel are a good option anyway, for several reasons. "Although they cost about $2 per square foot, rubber mats require much less bedding than what's needed on top of a dirt floor," he explains. "So, in a few years, rubber mats pay for themselves in bedding savings alone. Plus, less bedding means less dust in the air and less waste to haul out. Rubber mats are easy on a horse's legs and comfortable to sleep on. They also cut down the time and effort it takes to muck out the stall."

Fancier facilities often choose rubber brick flooring, "which looks great and provides superior traction in aisleways," says Woodford. "However, at $8.50 a square foot, I think rubber bricks are a little pricey for a stall. Rubber mats are just fine."

While it's easiest to prepare gravel beds for drainage in a new barn as the first phase of construction, you can still improve whatever's underfoot in the barn you have now. "Even if you've got a solid dirt floor, putting down rubber mats won't make matters any worse," Woodford points out. "They'll still reduce the bedding needed and the work involved in mucking out. If you'll also excavate each stall and shovel in some gravel under the mats, you'll have better drainage, a sweeter-smelling barn and much better air quality."

And now, light

"There's no reason to have a dark barn," Woodford says firmly. "Horses don't need artificial light, but they do need a lot of natural light during the daytime, just like we do. And there are many, many ways to let in light."

Lots of windows top the list. To reduce the risk of breakage, window panels should be plastic-based. "The best solution is glass-clad polycarbonate, which is plastic, lined with a thin layer of glass on both sides," says Woodford. "It's strong, too. You'd have a hard time breaking it with a baseball bat. Plexiglas, which scratches easily, ends up grimy and dingy-looking fairly quickly. Glass-clad polycarbonate, on the other hand, stays absolutely crystal clear forever, though it is more expensive."

Chenault Woodford focuses his equine architecture on the health, safety and comfort of horses.

It definitely doesn't come cheap, at about $26 a square foot, or $225 for a 3' x 3' window or door panel. The same panel of Plexiglas costs about $25. So if funds aren't plentiful, install Plexiglas now and replace it later with polycarbonate, a window at a time, as you can afford it. Laminated safety glass, like that used in some car windows, is another good alternative.

The next-best sources of light are dormers and big cupolas across the roofline, which let in light up high and illuminate everything below. On a metal roof, consider fiberglass skylights, which cost little more than regular metal panels.

Give 'em something to see

Being able to see is one thing, but being able to see movement is equally important. "Horses get bored in a dead-still environment," Woodford says. "Just like you'd hang a mobile above baby's crib, you should also give your horses something interesting to watch. That's why horses love Dutch doors — they can stick their heads out and look around, like a dog in a pickup truck." And because horses crave the companionship of other creatures, they need to be able to see other animals.

Stall grills, which let each horse easily see his neighbors, can greatly reduce the boredom and anxiety of stall life. "If your horse is an 'only child,' install a ceiling fan or get a goat or some barn cats, anything that moves," Woodford recommends. "Better yet, put in a window, where your horse can watch the world outside, even if that's only tractors or cars or birds going by. Otherwise, your horse is trapped in a visual prison, where nothing ever changes."

Quiet, please!

Loud, unexpected sounds can seriously distress a stall-bound horse. Loose doors banging in a storm and sleet rattling on a metal roof, for instance, are startling noises compared to wind rustling through trees or precipitation pattering on grass. Use an insulated roof to help mute even the pounding of hail, and install latches and hooks to keep doors and windows from whacking the building.

Feeding and watering

For your own sake, try to make your feeding setup as efficient and mess-free as possible. "Some horse owners wear business suits all day. But when they go home, they still have to feed the horses. Being able to feed and water quickly, without getting dirty or wet, can be quite convenient," Woodford observes. "Lazy-Susan-type feeders, which swing out into the barn aisle, are ideal. Or you can install small doors above the feed trough where you can just reach inside to dump in the feed."

Also consider installing automatic watering devices, which eliminate hauling a hose around, sloshing water and adding to barn humidity. Automatic waterers, however, can make it difficult to determine how much your horse is drinking, which can be important in monitoring his general health and well-being. Also, bored stall-bound horses often like to play with them and tear them up.

What's the best way to handle hay? "Well, whatever you do, don't store it above the stalls. A loft undermines some of your best opportunities for ventilation, since ceilings invariably trap ammonia fumes, dust and mold spores inside the stall. Lofts also block a lot of light. If you're trying to do things right, don't do a loft."

For clients who absolutely insist on a loft, Woodford reluctantly puts it over the aisleway, so flakes of hay can be dropped directly down into hay racks or stall mangers placed close to the front of the stalls. "This does save you from carrying hay to each stall and throwing it up into the rack," he says. "But, still, hay over the aisle adds lots of dust in the barn and that's simply not good for your horses."

Woodford says the best place to store hay is in a stall or, ideally, in a closed room to reduce dust. Use the same room to store bedding. Big sliding doors in that area, opening directly to the outside, are especially convenient, detouring delivery trucks from driving into the barn.

For optimum safety and ease of maintenance, barn aisles should be kept clear of things such as tack trunks, water faucets and saddle racks.

Details, details

Another key concern is hazard reduction, which often dovetails with adequate storage space. "Get rid of anything that sticks out into the aisle," Woodford insists. "Aisles should be clear all the way down — no wheelbarrows, no pitchforks, no tack hooks. Yes, everything has a place, but the aisleway isn't it.

"Also, water faucets and hydrants should be recessed into the walls, so that your horse doesn't bang his legs on them and you don't get your tack hung up as you walk by. Even little things, like tie rings, should be recessed. Hinged tie rings are great; they need a recess of only about a half-inch into the wall, where the ring swings down, out of harm's way."

To keep bored horses from rubbing their tails, Woodford recommends slanting the stall walls. "Let's say you have a four-foot solid wall with a grill on top. The bottom of the wall should be about a foot closer into the center of the stall than the top of the wall is," Woodford explains. "Even if a horse puts his feet right up against the bottom of the wall, his rump ends up almost a foot away from the wall. It's very difficult for a horse to sit back, keep his balance and rub side to side at that angle.

Warm water for washing is a particularly nice barn upgrade, for both you and your horse. If you're planning a new barn, but can't afford to put in a water heater right away, at least install the plumbing during construction. Ripping out walls later for electric wires and water pipes is messy and costly.

"Another nice low-cost item to have in your barn is a closed-circuit TV system, which is now more affordable than ever," Woodford says. "In any size barn, closed-circuit TVs are wonderfully convenient, since you can check on the horses from the house, at any time of day, without traipsing out to the barn. If you're handy, it's also a project you can do yourself with a little guidance from your local electronics store."

Also, don't forget to run a telephone line out to the barn. More than just a convenience for you, quick access to a phone — and to on-the-spot medical or veterinary advice — can be a lifesaver in emergencies.

Happily ever after

Of course, carefully considered design elements don't just affect a horse's physical health and comfort; they also directly influence his mental stability. An uncomfortable or anxious horse is more apt to develop stable vices, such as wood chewing, weaving or obsessive pawing. In turn, mental stress can contribute to physical ailments, particularly colic. "But even beyond all that, if your horse is happy, you'll enjoy him more," Woodford points out. "He'll be more responsive and easier to handle, and he'll relate to you better. All the things you want from your horse will be more likely to happen, if you're giving back as much as you can.

"My father was a horseman, and if he saw what people do in barns now, he'd say, 'What is the matter with these people? Horses don't need all that.' But, today, as animals who spend most of their day idle and cooped-up instead of pulling carts and herding cattle, horses actually need comfort and health factors in your barn. If you take care of those things, you have horses who are well-adapted and fun to be with. They enjoy life, and you enjoy life with them. And isn't that the whole point of having horses?" **PH**

5

A Home With Horses

*Living under the same roof as your horses
can be cozy and convenient. We'll give you guidelines
for the best house-barn combinations.*

For some people, maintaining both a house and a barn becomes too costly and time-consuming. For others, the hassle of schlepping back and forth between barn and home drains the pleasure from horsekeeping. For these and other reasons, some people choose to move in with their horses.

Actually, a house-barn combination can be comfortable and convenient when the human living quarters are designed with the same care and consideration most knowledgeable equestrians give to housing their horses.

However, a poorly planned house-barn can be a white elephant — miserable for both you and your horses and impossible to sell to anyone else. If there's any time where it truly pays to study the pros and cons and to avoid the pitfalls, building a house-barn is it. We talked to several house-barn builders, and a few residents as well, for the lowdown on bunking down in the barn.

Being able to check on horses late at night is important to many owners, particularly those with broodmares.

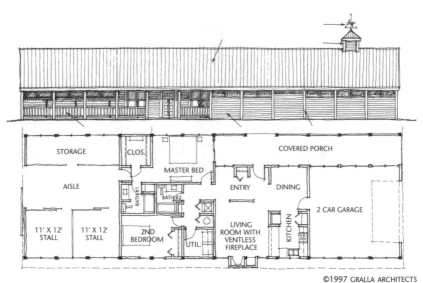

©1997 GRALLA ARCHITECTS

A small affordable home with attached stable that can be easily expanded as the need for additional space arises. With 1,344 square feet of living area, estimated cost of materials and construction is $80,000-$100,000.

Easy living

"Although I really love my horses, I hate rain, I hate cold, and I hate mud," says Kay Whittington, who moved into her Morton-built house-barn in Covington, Tenn., about two years ago. "I can walk out of my house, feed my horses, and turn them in or out, yet I never get wet or muddy. One night, when I had left my stallion out in his paddock, a nasty, gusting rainstorm blew up and I realized that with his stall door open, the rain would soak the barn. So here it is about 10 o'clock, and I'm already in my nightgown, but all I had to do was put on my boots, walk out into the barn, call my stallion and close him in the stall. I didn't even have to go outside."

Lorri Hayward, an accomplished horsewoman and owner of Hayward Design (which specializes in equine facilities), agrees that the convenience factor is one of the top advantages of living with your horses. "Think how much time you waste on the road," she points out. "The down side to living at the barn, though, is that sometimes you might feel that you can't get away from it. But, obviously, if you've made that kind of commitment, you're bitten by the horse bug big time."

Hayward also says that the effort and expense of maintaining separate buildings can be another motivation, as it was for one large remodeling project she worked on at a 100-stall boarding facility.

"The owners were spending all their time at the barn while paying someone to clean their house and mow their lawn. So we gutted a section of the barn that had previously housed some offices and a small tack store, and we remodeled the area into a nice home with a Greek Revival look, complete with a carriage porch in the front."

Cost savings can also be an advantage. Hayward is currently working on a project where the family already had house plans drawn up, as well as designs for a barn and arena. "But they discovered that to get everything they wanted for their horses, they couldn't afford the house. So now they've got a house-barn combination."

Bruce Brown, owner of Advance Barn Construction and who lives in a house-barn combination with his wife and nine horses, agrees that the savings can make a real difference. "If you compare the costs of building a separate house and barn with building an apartment-barn, then construction is often less, because you're combining some of the structural, electrical and plumbing costs."

The nitty gritty

Mention to your mom that you're thinking of moving into a barn, and you'll likely get a look of dismay. After all, only ardent horse lovers are tolerant of typical barn nuisances, such as flies, odors and dirt. But, those needn't be part of your well-planned home.

For instance, barn-builder Brown says that the first question people ask when they learn he lives in his barn is "How's the smell?" He answers, "No problem. If it's done correctly, with proper ventilation and layout, there are no barn smells in the house. In our house, we go from the barn into the tack room with a sealed door; then we have another hallway that goes up to our living area, where there's another door. We hang our barn clothes in the hallway before coming into the house. That cuts down on the dirt and dust."

Another house-barn resident adds, "When I first built my place, I tried to get away without putting in a fly-control system. That was foolish — the house stayed full of flies all the time, despite having clean stalls. So I put in a fly-spray system and ended that problem."

Our barn-building experts offered a few other tips to keep your barn home relatively spick and span:

■ Keeping barn aisles swept and walls washed will reduce the tracking in of dirt and drifting in of dust.

■ In addition to buffer zones between the barn and house, high-quality doors with good seals will help keep down dust infiltration.
■ Plan the barn's ventilation system to pull air (laden with dust) away from living areas.
■ Conscientious stall-cleaning will cut way down on odors and flies.

Quiet, please?

Another common concern when living with horses is the noise. Of course, the easiest way to cut down on noise is to not build your living spaces above the stalls and to provide buffer zones (such as tack or feed rooms) between the stall area and the house. Bob Thiel, with Walters Buildings, says another key to noise reduction is good insulation in walls between the house and the barn area.

Then, again, some horse owners find comfort in being within earshot of their horses. "Most people who live in a house-barn want to hear the noises that tell you something's wrong," says Brown, who speaks from personal experience. "You get used to the every-day noises, like neighing and stall-door banging."

Design details

By keeping several key design principles in mind while you plan your house-barn, you can avoid many — if not all — the primary problems that plague thrown-together structures.

Check local fire and construction codes. *Special restrictions may apply to multi-use buildings. Also, local government may consider a large barn a commercial facility (or a potential place of assembly), and public safety factors must be considered.*

Building site. *Consider the building site carefully, especially in terms of manure, storage, drainage and wind direction during different seasons.*

Build only the space you need now. *"In many cases, we recommend less than what our clients originally consider building," says Todd Gralla. "It's common for people to overestimate their needs. For instance, people with 12* mares may want a 20-stall broodmare barn because they plan to later expand the herd. But why build a 20-stall barn that you have to clean and maintain right now, if you're not going to need it for a few years? Plan the barn to be easily modified later."

Do not put human living spaces over horse stalls. Horses need ventilation, and people need insulation. To preserve good ventilation for your horses (which means keeping an open, vaulted area above the stalls), design your living spaces beside the barn or above barn-service areas, such as tack and feed rooms, wash bays, garage and barn office.

Build buffer zones between the house and stalls. Dennis Rusch, design estimator for Morton Buildings, says that when designing the residence adjacent to the barn, where everything is on the ground-floor level, you should try to put a feed room or tack room between the last stall and the living quarters. This will give you a buffer from sounds, smells, dust and flies. You can also create buffers by designing your living quarters so that closets, hallways or bathrooms — instead of your bedroom or kitchen — are next to stall or service-room walls.

A pleasing split-rail fence and window boxes with colorful flowers help make this house-barn as "homey" for humans as for horses.

No direct entries from stall area into the home. Put
house entries in hallways or stairwells leading from a
separately enclosed barn service area (such as the office
or tack room), never directly from the stable area. Create
transitional rooms where you can leave your mucky boots
or dusty chaps outside your clean living space.

Store bulk bedding and hay in a separate structure.
You'll reduce your fire hazard, improve the air quality for
your horses and reduce the amount of dust that finds its
way into your home. You may also improve your insurance rating.

Consider adding a guest bath in the barn. If you plan to
have boarders or lots of barn guests, include a half-bath
with a toilet and sink in the barn area to keep extra activity out of the house.

Dollars and sense

Depending on your budget and needs, you can spend as little as
$80,000 on a 1,200-square-foot home with a covered garage and two-
stall barn, or as much as several million dollars for a combined 3,000-
square-foot luxury home/10-stall barn/indoor arena (both projects
of Stan Gralla Architects). Bruce Brown has even built a $60,000
combination with three stalls and a one-room studio apartment.

But beyond cost, there are several other issues you must consider before breaking ground. First and foremost, as Dennis Rusch with
Morton Buildings says bluntly, "There's a limited resale market for
this type of structure. So, knowing that you might end up stuck with
your house-barn, talk to people who already live in a house-barn to
see exactly what it entails and if it really fits your lifestyle.

Also, obtaining financing can be tough. "Banks often balk at lend-
ing money on this type of structure because it doesn't conform to
the Fannie Mae and Freddie Mac guidelines set up in the residen-
tial-housing industry," says Brown. "A house-barn, in most cases,
is considered a mixed-use building, which is not covered under normal residential loans. Often, you'll need to find a local bank or in-
stitution that keeps some of their loans in-house, instead of trying
to sell them on the secondary market. They'll also often require a
bigger down payment, maybe as much as 25 or 30 percent."

Resale considerations are crucial when planning any residence, but especially with house-barn combinations. Be sure to select the site carefully and position the structure to take full advantage of surrounding scenery.

Of course, if you have lots of assets and leverage, borrowing may be no big deal. Otherwise, you may need to present the bank with a business plan or an explanation of other options and revenue-producing possibilities for such a property. Brown suggests planning your facility so that, if you do need to sell, the barn areas can be converted to more living space (such as an office, studio, workshop or garage) without a lot of extra expense.

In fact, that's how he designed his own house-barn, which currently has about 1,800 square feet of living space, but could easily be converted to a 5,000-square-foot home without the stalls and barn areas.

Whittington says the biggest problem she's had is trying to get affordable insurance. "Because the house and barn are attached, they insure the entire place at the risk value of the barn."

Keep in mind, that even if you take all appropriate fire-hazard reductions, you may still live in a high-risk category zone, especially if you live out in the country.

Brown suggests that house-barn residents should seek out firms who know how to insure horse facilities, instead of the more familiar big-name insurance companies.

One more caveat

Bob Johnson, a professional Quarter Horse trainer, lives with his wife in a lovely house-barn in Dickson, Tenn. While he loves his home and the convenience of being able to keep a close eye on his valuable "roommates," he does point out that, at a business barn where customers visit, the primary drawback of the house-barn arrangement is the lack of privacy. "It's hard to separate your professional life from your personal life when you live and work at the same location," he comments. "No matter who drives in, you're there. You never get a chance to be alone." **PH**

6

A Breath Of Fresh Air

*Confining a horse to a dank,
musty barn can be more hazardous to his health
than leaving him outside in bad weather.*

Air quality has a direct effect on a horse's health. Stagnant, contaminant-laden air can cause respiratory illnesses, chronic coughing and decreased lung function, resulting in poor performance. Equine experts agree: Ventilation is one of the most important factors in assuring a healthy habitat for your horse.

A barn is an artificial environment for a horse. By nature, horses are outdoor creatures, accustomed to a continuous supply of fresh, clean air. "If they had a choice, horses would not live indoors," says Todd Gralla, marketing director for Stan Gralla Architects, one of the country's leading firms for equine-facility designs. "In any building, no matter how clean, there's an abundance of airborne particulate matter, even if we can't see it."

That matter — dust from hay, mold from dampness, ammonia fumes from urine — can compromise a horse's lungs. Spilled feed and soiled bedding can be a prime breeding ground for fungal growth, bacteria and mold, increasing susceptibility to allergies and respiratory diseases. Airborne irritants can also aggravate — or even cause — conditions such as chronic obstructive pulmonary disease, more commonly called "heaves." Long-term exposure can eventually lead to permanent lung damage.

"Good ventilation in the barn is important for several reasons," says Susan Raymond, an aerobiology researcher at the Equine Research Centre (ERC) in Guelph, Ontario, Canada. "Ventilation improves air quality by diluting and reducing horses' exposure to contaminants. It also helps keep the bedding drier, which will help reduce mold."

Good air flow will also reduce ammonia levels, which can damage a horse's respiratory system and make him more vulnerable to infectious agents and respiratory illnesses. In addition, proper ventilation can help keep the barn cooler in summer, reduce mildew on tack and other surfaces, and help keep the barn interior drier and sweeter-smelling, attracting fewer flies. In the long run, investing in ventilation saves money.

How much air is enough?

In a well-ventilated barn, irritant-laden air is constantly replaced with clean, fresh air. Although many experts suggest at least four air exchanges per hour, the ERC recommends between eight and 10 air changes per hour. Raymond explains, "In general, four air changes are sufficient for any type of livestock. However, what we expect from a horse is very different from what we expect from a cow or chicken, in terms of long life, reproduction and athletic performance. To maintain their health, horses need a higher ventilation rate than other livestock."

Chenault Woodford, senior partner at the architectural firm of CMW, Inc., in Lexington, Ky., agrees. "Look at standards for humans," he points out. "In a restaurant or school classroom, most

A cupola (below) can be an efficient ventilation companion to ridge vents and/or monitor roofs (top). As hot air rises and escapes, it causes cooler air close to the ground to be drawn into the barn. Thus, not only does the heat escape, cooling the barn, but the air circulates as well.

building codes require six air changes per hour. Public restrooms require 15 air changes per hour. Well, a stall is a horse's living room, dining room, bedroom and bathroom. So, although the minimum is four changes per hour, more would be much better. Remember that outside, where horses normally live, there may be as many as 200 air changes per hour, depending on wind movement."

In this barn, air flow is not obstructed by a loft. Hot air rises and escapes through ridge vents, which are barely noticeable.

Because high heat is harder on horses than cold temperatures, air flow is critical for stall-bound horses in summer. Ventilation is equally important in winter, however, when horses often spend more time indoors. A common mistake that well-meaning horseowners make is assuming their horses are cozy in the same kind of snug surroundings as we are. But when you close all doors and windows and seal up every crack, you also trap air pollution inside. Air exchanges must continue year-round.

Unfortunately, it's tough for the typical horseowner to tell how many air exchanges he's getting. If you're still concerned, however, after implementing the suggestions below, the ERC does have a complicated physics formula that can help. "Barn owners are welcomed to call us and let us punch their numbers into our computer (fee about $25) for an assessment," Raymond says.

Natural or mechanical?

Most experts recommend avoiding mechanical ventilation (fans and exhaust systems) whenever possible. "In a large barn, to equal the amount of air flow provided by well-designed natural ventilation, a fan would make so much noise that neither horse nor man would ever want to set foot in that building," says Woodford. "It would also use a lot of electrical power. Instead, with careful planning, natural ventilation can be adequate for the great majority of barns, in any weather."

Even on a windless day, a properly designed barn can make an inside breeze. Thermal convection currents are created by air warmed by the barn's absorption of solar heat or, in winter, by body heat radiating from the horses. Warm air rises, taking with it water vapors, particulate matter and heat. If there are adequate outlets up high, the hot air escaping creates a vacuum below, which pulls cooler air inside via open doors, windows and other inlets. "With sufficient inlets and outlets, you can create air flow inside your building, with absolutely no air movement outside," says Woodford.

You can also take advantage of natural breezes by aligning your barn to catch prevailing winds. As wind flows down the center aisle, it creates a negative pressure; with open windows and doors in each stall, that negative pressure will pull air through the stalls and out into the aisle. With a balanced air flow, stalls will be aerated more efficiently, with fewer pockets of stale, dead-still air.

Signs of poor ventilation

If you're soon sneezing or coughing after you walk into a barn, you can bet the air in there is harming the horses, too. Horses spend much more time in the barn than we do, so they're exposed to irritants a lot longer. Signs of a poorly ventilated barn include:

■ *A strong smell of ammonia.*

■ *Horses with chronic coughs or constant watery nasal discharges.*

■ *Condensation on inside surfaces.*

■ *Damp stalls, with moisture buildup or mold in bedding.*

■ *Excessive dust on windows and cobwebs on walls.*

■ *Noticeable temperature differences from one part of the barn to another. If some areas (especially stalls) seem warmer than others, for instance, that means air isn't circulating through the whole barn, leaving pockets of stagnant air.*

Maximizing air movement

If you're selecting a site for a new barn, make sure it won't be blocked from summer breezes by other buildings or hillsides. Also, don't site it in a low spot that drains poorly (i.e., more humidity, dampness and mold inside).

The design of the barn is also key. The pitch of your barn roof can dramatically enhance — or hinder — convection currents. Barn experts recommend at least a 6:12 pitch, which means six inches of rise for every 12 inches of lateral distance (an angle of about 27 degrees), but check your local building codes.

"In any barn, the warm air will rise and accumulate at the highest part of the barn," says Gralla. "The pitch of your roof works like a chimney in your house. A steeper pitch will better funnel the air, increasing your rate of ventilation; with a flat roof, the warm air is spread over a wide area, which slows it down."

Exterior stall doors and windows allow horses to breathe fresh air as well as to enjoy watching the outside activities.

Of course, hay lofts drastically reduce air flow. An open interior not only allows freer movement of stale air out of stalls, but it also reduces the amount of dust and debris falling into the stalls from above. If you must have a loft, Raymond recommends installing "chimneys" to act as outlets so air can escape from below, up through the loft to the outside.

Mesh panels or grilled partitions around stall perimeters can also help facilitate air flow. For quality stall components that maximize ventilation, many barn builders turn to custom barn manufacturers, such as Kentucky-based Lucas Equine Equipment. Some of the company's most popular products are its heavy-mesh screen doors for inside and out, allowing air flow directly across the bottom of the stall. "We've even done complete stall systems with open mesh across the front," says Don Floyd, Lucas' sales manager. "At the bottom of the mesh screen, we put a bedding guard, which is a 12-inch solid steel panel to keep straw or shavings in the stall."

Ventilation's partner — insulation

Insulation and ventilation go hand-in-hand in moderating your barn's indoor climate. Insulation helps reduce heat gain in summer, heat loss in the winter and condensation year-round. However, if you over-insulate your barn, you'll reduce your ability to maximize natural ventilation. "The more insulation you have, the less temperature differential you'll have, which means your ability to make an artificial wind through thermal convection currents also diminishes," Woodford explains. "So, the better insulated your barn is, the more likely you'll need mechanical ventilation. You have to consider your extreme seasons and decide which one you'll address which way."

For instance, if you're building in a cold northern climate, you want a lot of insulation to hold in heat. "But the farther south you go, the less insulation you need, because you're not that concerned about cold winters and you want a temperature differential to create an air current," he says. "As far as condensation, if you've got good ventilation, air movement will carry it away as water vapor."

This way out

Of course, for efficient natural ventilation, hot air rising to the top of the barn must have an escape route. Ridge vents and cupolas are the most commonly selected outlets.

A continuous ridge vent runs the entire length of the roof. Like a bridge, it spans and covers a gap in the roof's peak, running along both sides of the ridge beam. A vent cap allows hot air to escape out the top of the roof, while keeping rain from getting in. Low-profile ridge vents are hardly noticeable from the ground.

Many companies make prefabricated ridge vents, available at large building supply companies. Woodford cautions, "A residential ridge vent, often used on house attics, only offers about a 1" slot, which isn't enough. Barns need bigger industrial-type ridge vents."

Two firms that make ridge vents specifically for barns are Plyco Corporation and Cannon Ball. Woodford estimates that on a 70-foot-long roof, a standard industrial ridge vent will cost about $500.

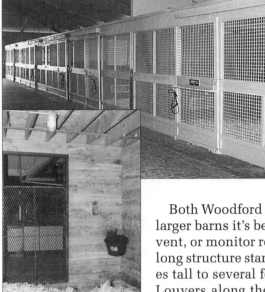

Great for air flow, mesh-panel stalls allow you to keep a watchful eye on horses inside. But in lieu of expensive stall doors, consider using stall guards for well-behaved residents.

Both Woodford and Gralla agree that for larger barns it's better to have a structural vent, or monitor roof, which is basically a long structure standing from several inches tall to several feet above the roof peak. Louvers along the side tilt down to prevent rain from entering. "With taller monitor roofs, windows along the sides can also let in light," Woodford says. "In the era before mechanical ventilation, more attention was paid to natural ventilation, so you'll often see monitor roofs on old barns and industrial buildings."

Built on-site as part of the overall roof structure, a monitor roof about 40 feet long and two feet high would cost about $3,200, Woodford estimates. "However, a monitor roof will be at least four times as effective as an industrial ridge vent," he says. "And, because it's spread out across the roof, it works as well as cupolas, which cost considerably more."

Picturesque barn spires frequently topped with weather vanes, cupolas are chimney-like roof vents. Like monitor roofs, most have louvers to repel precipitation; large ones often incorporate windows.

Many cupolas, Woodford says, are simply too small to do much good. "The bigger you make a cupola, the better it is. For a 40' x 70' barn, I'd put on a 12' x 12' cupola about six feet high. The most convenient ones have motorized windows, where you can push a switch to modulate the amount of opening. One that size with motorized windows would probably cost about $20,000."

As the barn gets longer, however, one cupola will benefit only a limited area of the barn. So you'll also need a ridge vent, a monitor roof or more cupolas.

Raymond points out that the type of building often determines the best option: "A ridge vent is better for an open-ceiling barn without an enclosed loft. But a barn with a loft across the stalls and aisle will need chimneys and cupolas."

Ventilated skylights are another option for loftless barns. Velux-America makes several sizes with high-performance insulated glass, ranging in cost from $274 to $477. The most popular size, 2' x 4', costs $314. Available accessories include weather-tight flashing systems for both metal and shingled roofs, electric systems that will open the vents at the touch of a button, and a full line of shading devices. Deluxe models include rain sensors, which will automatically close the vents in inclement weather.

Cutting down on airborne contaminants

Several factors, of course, affect the amount of ventilation you need — your barn can have an efficient air flow, but if you're constantly filling the air with contaminants, you're counteracting your ventilation efforts. Conscientious stable-management practices can significantly improve air quality:

■ *Repair any water leaks. Mold thrives in chronic damp spots. Make a conscious effort to reduce water sloshed in stalls or in the aisleway.*

■ *Improve stall-floor drainage to reduce dampness, and use hydrated lime or a commercial stall odor-absorber to neutralize ammonia from urine.*

■ *Soak hay in water before feeding it. Dry hay can release enormous amounts of lung-irritating particles into the air. Also, don't drop hay into stalls from a loft. Carry the hay into each horse's stall.*

■ *Purchase the best-quality, least-dusty hay and bedding you can afford. If possible, avoid straw bedding, which is especially susceptible to mold. Store hay and bedding in a separate room or building, away from stalls (a good idea for reducing fire hazards, too).*

■ *Remove your horse from the barn while you sweep the barn aisle, muck the stalls or spread new bedding. Let the dust settle before you bring him back in.*

■ *Keep stalls clean. Manure buildup encourages the growth of fungus and bacteria, while decomposing bedding can release irritating fumes. Also, distance the manure pile away from the barn, to reduce particulate matter blowing back into the barn.*

This way in

To work properly, a ventilation system needs air flow into the barn as well as out of it. Raymond recommends at least twice as much inlet area as outlet area. As a general rule of thumb, the ERC recommends a minimum of 3.23 square feet of inlet area per horse and 1.08 square feet of outlet area.

"Of course, you must consider the size of your building as well," Raymond comments. "If you only have two horses in a very big barn, with only the minimum recommended inlet and outlet space for two horses, the air may not distribute evenly. Also, it's much better to have a large number of small inlets than one big inlet. With lots of smaller inlets, more air will circulate throughout the whole barn and the air exchange will be more evenly distributed."

In addition to lots of doors and windows, wall vents provide an excellent source for incoming air. Keep in mind, the bigger the height difference between your inlets and outlets, the better ventilation rate you'll get. So some builders position wall vents in the stall about eight inches off the stall floor: air enters low, warms and then rises, pulling odors and contaminants from the bottom up.

Raymond points out two cautions about wall vents. First, be sure inner openings have sturdy mesh or very small louvers to keep hooves from getting caught. Second, if they're not constructed properly to diffuse incoming air, wall vents can create drafts in winter. "To help prevent drafts," she says, "reduce the speed and force of incoming air. It's better for the inlet to be hinged from the bottom, directing air upward, so the cool air will enter and sink slowly, instead of blow down directly on the horse."

In areas prone to flies, mosquitoes and pesky birds (carriers of diseases), put small-mesh screens on all windows, doors and inlets. If you plan to keep stall windows open frequently, you may also want to consider incorporating roof overhangs to help block rain.

Retrofitting an older barn

"The biggest problem we find in most existing barns is mainly the roof pitch. Also, most barns go up to a sealed-off ridge, with no way for air to escape," Gralla points out.

Although replacing an entire roof structure is probably too costly for many barn owners, he says, modifying an existing roof with a ridge vent or other outlets is certainly possible. Most major roof modifications, however, aren't good do-it-yourself projects. To avoid leaks from rain, installing ridge vents, structural vents and cupolas is best left to professional contractors, he suggests.

If money is tight, turbine vents are an inexpensive last option. Like small round metal "cupolas," turbine vents operate with inner fan blades that catch outside breezes and, while spinning, pull hot air out of the barn. Again, several smaller turbines evenly spaced along the roof are more effective than one large one in the middle or at one end. "But any opening is better than none," Gralla states.

Replacing solid stall fronts and partitions with mesh screen or bar grills is "the biggest thing you can do to open up a barn inside," Gralla says. Also, consider adding windows and/or outside doors to each stall. If you can't afford that, stall guards can at least allow you to leave stall doors open while keeping your horses safely confined inside.

Despite your best efforts, if your roof has a shallow pitch or if you're in an extremely hot, humid climate, you may still be stuck with using fans. Just be certain you're working with Mother Nature, instead of against her. "With any mechanical methods, you always want to work with the basic principles of good ventilation," says Raymond. "With box fans or ceiling fans, be sure you've got them pointed the right way. You don't want to push hot air down and stir up dust and mold spores; instead, you want to pull cool air up. And, instead of putting in a big fan to blow a breeze down the aisleway, you should put an exhaust fan in the chimney to draw hot air out."

Gralla agrees, saying it's important to use the laws of mechanics correctly. "We've seen structures with exhaust fans on each end, both blowing inside air out, which just creates a vacuum where air goes nowhere. If you're going to use two exhaust fans, one should bring air in, and one should blow air out. You've got to have air flow." ■PH

7

Fighting Fire

Filled with flammable materials,
horse barns are often a spark away from tragedy.
With prevention, preparation and the right products,
you can protect your horses.

Our horses' homes are filled with flammables, from hay and bedding to horse blankets. It's simply a fact of common horsekeeping — barns are big combustibles just waiting to ignite. In fact, the National Equine Safety Association (NESA) estimates that the over 5,000 barn fires a year — more than 14 per day, across the country— kill more horses than all natural disasters combined. Most barn fires, however, are preventable with hazard reduction, routine maintenance and fire-suppression products.

Sound the alarm

Early detection of any fire can save lives and property. Unfortunately, horse barns present significant challenges for alarm systems, according to Alfred Longhitano, chairman of the National Fire Prevention Association's Technical Committee for Fire Prevention in Racetrack Stables and vice president of Gage-Babcock & Associates, a consulting engineering firm that specializes in fire protection.

Longhitano explains that standard ionization smoke detectors often malfunction in a barn environment, either clogging up from dirt or setting off false alarms triggered by dust or condensation. Even sophisticated optical smoke-detector systems, which are activated when visible smoke particles deflect a light beam inside the detector, can be hypersensitive in a barn.

RED HEAD BRASS PHOTO

Design using two 45° elbows

Fighting a barn fire requires lots of water. With a dry hydrant, illustrated below, your nearby farm pond could supply that need.

A heat detector is a better option, but even then you must choose the right kind. There are three basic types of heat detectors, according to Longhitano: **fixed-temperature detectors**, which activate when the surrounding temperature reaches a certain level; **rate-of-rise detectors**, which activate when they sense an abnormally fast rate of temperature increase; and **rate-compensating thermal detectors**, which combine both technologies.

"Rate-compensating thermal detectors give you the stability of the fixed-temperature detector, with a little more of the speed of the rate-of-rise detector, so they're more dependable," Longhitano points out. "Plus, they survive pretty well in corrosive environments, making them effective in a barn." Longhitano estimates that the rate-compensating thermal detectors cost about $40 to $50 each, not counting a control panel or monitoring system.

Of course, an alarm does no good if no one hears it. So, any system you install should include hook-up to a monitored area — either to your home or, better yet, to a 24-hour monitoring service that will contact the fire department when you're away.

Extinguishing the flames

In most barn fires, your first priorities should be to (1) evacuate all humans, (2) call the fire department, (3) evacuate horses, but ONLY if the fire is still small and there's no risk to your own safety, and (4) try to put out the fire. Because a barn is so highly combustible, there's no way to predict how fast a small fire may burst into an inferno.

You wouldn't want a small, isolated, easily contained fire to spread unchecked, however, if you had the means to quickly and safely stop it. While you may instinctively reach for a water hose, some fires — gas, oil and electrical, for instance — are more dangerous when mixed with water (you can get electrocuted trying to fight an electrical fire with water, and water can cause flaming oil to splatter and spread). Whenever possible, your first line of defense should be a general-purpose fire extinguisher.

"If you can catch a fire while it's still smoldering and hasn't burst into such a body of flame that it drives you away, and if you can knock it back with a fire extinguisher, the chances of buying enough time to evacuate the horses increase tremendously," says Longhitano. "What we say in the fire-fighting field is, 'The first few seconds are yours; the next few hours belong to the fire.' Those first few seconds are critical."

Fire extinguishers are rated for the type of fire each is appropriate to fight.

■ **Type A** extinguishers will douse a fire fueled by common combustibles (hay, wood, paper, plastics, rubber).
■ **Type B** extinguishers will snuff out fires fueled by gasoline, grease and oil.
■ **Type C** extinguishers are required for electrical fires (wiring, fuse box, appliances, etc.).

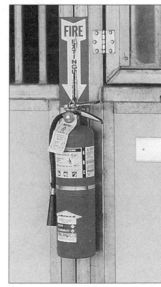

Fire experts suggest mounting several extinguishers throughout the barn in highly visible locations along the aisleway, in the tack room and near hay storage, plus one just inside each barn entrance.

Since barn fires can be fueled by any and all of the above, your best bet is a multipurpose ABC-rated fire extinguisher that can be used on all types of fires. Look for models with metal caps, not plastic, which can melt in heat.

Longhitano recommends at least one extinguisher for every 2,000 square feet of space, so that you're never more than 75 feet from an extinguisher.

Then, clean and inspect each extinguisher once a month, he says, checking the gauges for correct pressurization; fire extinguishers can lose pressure over time, so you may need to have them recharged annually (call your local fire department for advice).

Also, take the time to practice with an extinguisher before an emergency. Take one out and discharge it in the yard. See how you have to aim it to hit a target, and see how the stuff comes out, what the pattern looks like, how far it reaches. You learn a lot by actually discharging one. Then, have your practice extinguisher recharged before you mount it for duty.

Calling in the pros

One of the most valuable — and least expensive — proactive steps you can take for fighting a future barn fire is to invite the fire department out before you need them. Enlist their assistance in mapping out an evacuation plan; later, practice a mock evacuation with your horses in the dark, in a non-frantic atmosphere, to check for kinks in the plan.

A friendly tour will not only familiarize your local fire fighters with the location and layout of your farm, but can also help answer a number of critical questions:

■ *In an emergency, what is their estimated response time? How long will you be on your own?*

■ *Is your farm driveway and address well-marked, easy to spot in the dark?*

■ *Is access to your facility adequate? Can a large fire truck get to the barn? Is the driveway wide enough and straight enough, with adequate turnarounds? What about locked gates or load ratings of private bridges?*

> ■ *Where are available water hydrants and/or alternate water sources?*
>
> *Finally, post highly visible emergency phone numbers near the telephone. Keep a laminated map of the barn — marking all stalls, aisleways and exits — near the main exit for quick reference for fire fighters. In a place away from the barn, keep a list of animals, with their markings and identification characteristics, along with clear photographs, in case they escape during the chaos.*

Sprinklers to the rescue

A barn can be fully involved within 90 seconds of a smoldering fire breaking into flames. Without immediate suppression efforts, you may have little chance of saving anything. That's where automatic suppression systems — fire sprinklers — can mean the difference between life and death for your horses.

"Automatic sprinkler systems are the best means of protecting animals and barns — not to mention the people who risk their lives trying to evacuate the animals," Longhitano says firmly. "As soon as heat from the fire activates the sprinkler head, water starts dousing the flames. Also, once water starts to flow, there's usually a switch in the main pipe that activates a fire alarm. So now you've combined detection capability with fire suppression — it's like having a fireman standing right there, ready with a hose."

The primary problem with automatic sprinklers, however, is that they must have adequate water pressure. "Unfortunately, most rural stables don't have the benefit of town water," says Steven P. Wilson, president of Hampshire Development and Stock Safe automatic fire suppression systems, "and a well-water system won't supply enough pressure for even one sprinkler head."

Well pumps, Wilson says, typically supply only five to 10 gallons of water a minute, but just one sprinkler head needs about 20 to 25 gallons per minute. With one sprinkler head protecting an area about 10' x 10', a full fire sprinkler system for a relatively small barn can easily demand 300 to 400 gallons a minute.

When Wilson built his own barn several years ago, he decided to solve that problem. Today, his Stock Safe fire suppression system uses water stored in large underground holding tanks, along with compressed nitrogen, which supplies the pressure for the sprinkler system.

"The important thing is that this system works with no supporting equipment — you can have no electric power, no city or well water and no phone service, yet this system still works," says Wilson. "It will immediately contact the fire department, off radio control with battery back-up, no matter what, and it will deliver the water, no matter what."

Other fire-suppression companies, like Brown Sprinkler Corporation, use systems with single tanks that store water and compressed air together. "Basically, you fill a large steel storage tank about two-thirds full of water, and you have an air compressor that pumps in compressed air into the other third of the tank, with a switch that maintains the pressure," Longhitano says.

Choosing the size of your water storage tank (i.e., how much you'll have to pay for it), says Longhitano, is a risk-management decision. "You must decide what you're trying to accomplish with the sprinkler system — how much time are you trying to buy with it? It doesn't take too long for five or six sprinklers to open in a barn fire. If five or six sprinklers are discharging an average of 20 gallons per minute each, that's 100 to 120 gallons per minute.

"If you're depending on fire fighters to evacuate your horses, how long will it take for them to get there? If it'll take 20 minutes, and your system is putting out 120 gallons per minute, you'll need 2,400 gallons of water. If there's always someone around the barn, however, you may only need a few minutes to save the horses, so you'd need less water."

Unfortunately, due to the complicated nature of automatic sprinkler systems that depend on underground water storage (and the huge amount of labor involved), costs can be high. Wilson estimates, for instance, that a Stock Safe system for a one-story 70' x 40' barn (with no loft) would cost from $12,000 to $15,000, including the water and nitrogen tanks, alarms and sprinkler system.

Yet, your money is undoubtedly well-spent on a sprinkler system, say both Longhitano and Wilson, simply because it takes so much of the burden off of you. Wilson says, "With a fire-suppression system, you don't have to worry — the sprinkler will fight the fire better than you can, the fire department is already on the way, and you can get your horses out."

Built-in protection

■ *Be sure the barn layout includes several exits; smarter yet, design all stalls with both indoor and outdoor doors, for quick evacuation, and make sure your horse is familiar with using all exits regularly.*

■ *Locate the barn's main electrical panel in the driest, least dusty area of the barn, and keep it clean and free of surrounding clutter. Be sure to install enough power and circuit breakers to prevent overload.*

■ *Encase electrical wires in metal conduit to deter gnawing rodents and/or horses. All electrical outlets should have covers to protect them from dust and moisture.*

■ *Where possible, replace incandescent light bulbs with cooler-burning fluorescent lights.*

■ *Ensure a good ventilation system that will help reduce accumulation of dust and cobwebs, as well as reduce heat buildup in summer.*

■ *Install only UL-approved electrical appliances, such as fence chargers and water heaters.*

■ *If you must store some hay and bedding in the barn, construct a special storage area as far away from the stalls as possible, enclosed with a two-hour fire-resistant wall and roof materials.*

■ *Be sure your farm plans include a safely fenced area nearby — such as a round pen or paddock — for temporarily securing evacuated horses.*

Sparks from a shattered light bulb could start a fire, and the broken glass injure your horse. Enclosing light fixtures in wire cages or globes provide an added safety measure.

Water, water, anywhere

By the time the fire department arrives, most likely what's still burning are the type A combustibles — the hay, the bedding, the barn itself. At that point, fire fighting efforts require water, lots and lots of water.

Many horse owners, though, live far from municipal water lines and fire hydrants, which means fire-fighting efforts could be limited to only the amount of water a fire tanker can bring with it (typically from 750 to 2,000 gallons). The NESA points out that fighting a hay fire of 250 bales, however, takes 500 gallons of water per minute. If you're fortunate enough to live near a lake, pond, river or stream, consider installing a **dry hydrant** to make that water immediately available to the fire department.

Richard Zerrer, product engineer with Red Head Brass, explains that a dry hydrant uses a relatively simple system of six-inch PVC piping — one end runs underground into a nearby water source (like a pond or stream), and the other end stands up a couple of feet above the ground, about 10 to 15 feet away from the water, with a standard fire-department connection. In the event of a barn fire, the fire truck can quickly pull up to the hydrant, connect a hose and start pumping.

"When installed correctly, our Maxi-Flow dry hydrant system can produce 1,000 gallons a minute," says Zerrer, "which is even more than what a city hydrant produces, because of the size of the piping." And, although fire departments can toss out their own equipment to siphon water from a pond or pool (in lieu of a municipal hydrant), Zerrer says a dry hydrant can deliver about five times as much water.

Materials for a Maxi-Flow dry hydrant cost about $500 to $600; excavation and installation charges depend on local labor rates.

Fire retardants

If you're planning to build a new barn or expand/renovate an existing barn, using **fire-retardant-treated wood (FRTW)** can be a smart investment. Pressure impregnated with chemicals that reduce flame spread and smoke FRTW isn't totally noncombustible — it eventually will burn.

"In a barn built of fire-retardant-treated wood, if a fire started in straw up against a corner, for example, that corner will scorch, and

FRTW isn't totally noncombustible — if subjected to a flame long enough, it will burn. But it can buy you precious time to evacuate your horses.

HOOVER TREATED WOOD COMPANY PHOTO

the fire from the straw may consume that wood," says Ray Miller with Hoover Treated Wood. "However, once the straw has burned, the fire will not continue to burn and spread throughout the barn."

Miller says an important distinction in selecting FRTW for horse barns is that "interior" formulations (unexposed to weather) are leechable. Though the chemicals are non-toxic, they lose their fire-retardant qualities when exposed to moisture.

A better option for horse barns, Miller suggests, would be an exterior formulation, which is more expensive, but impervious to high humidity and kicked-over water buckets.

Of course, FRTW is significantly more expensive than non-treated lumber (call your local lumber yard for quotes), and don't forget to add shipping. Even if you can't afford FRTW for your entire barn, seriously consider it for structural supports and roof trusses — the longer a burning barn remains standing, the longer you'll have to evacuate horses.

Longhitano mentions one caveat, though — if you opt for trusses made of FRTW, check construction carefully. "Many trusses today use metal gusset plates that join the wood," he says. "If you heat up the gusset plate, the wood around the nails weakens and chars, and if the gusset plates let go, then the truss collapses, even though the wood itself may not have burned away."

Let's say that your current barn is already built of regular, non-treated lumber. You can still buy yourself some extra time by applying a flame-retardant coating.

According to Betty Tomlin, with Flame Control Coatings Inc., fire-retardant coatings are classified according to their ability to withstand surface burning (when subjected to heat, the coating foams up and forms a sponge-like protective barrier between the flame and the substrate). In a bad fire, a flame-retardant coating won't save your barn — its main purpose is to slow the fire down long enough to give you time to evacuate your horses.

Classifications are based on rates of flame spread; the lower the flame-spread rate, the better. As a reference point, uncoated woods typically have flame-spread ratings of about 100 to 110. A Class A flame-retardant coating will have a flame-spread rating of 0 to 25; a Class B coating has a rating of 26 to 75.

Flame Control's Class A wood paint #20-20, for instance, has a flame-spread rating of 10, which reduces surface-burning characteristics by 90 percent. If you prefer wood's natural tones, the company also makes varnish systems (requiring a basecoat and topcoat). Because the Class A varnish is susceptible to moisture and humidity, however, Tomlin recommends Flame Control's Class B product for horse barns. "Our Class B varnish system is every bit as durable as any conventional alkyd varnish," she says, "plus its flame-spread rating of 45 reduces surface burning by 55 percent."

"Additionally, anyone who knows how to paint can apply these products," says Tomlin. "Most can be brushed on, but we recommend spraying, since you get a more uniform finish that way."

Fire-retardant coatings are sold by single gallon, in five-gallon pails and in 55-gallon drums, and most paint stores can special order whatever you need. Be prepared, though — the products are pricey. At Sherwin-Williams, for instance, Flame Control's Class A paint #20-20 is about $50 per gallon, and a single gallon only covers 190 to 200 square feet (as compared to an average gallon of paint that covers about 600 square feet). Also, with just about any fire-retardant coating, you'll need to reapply it every three to five years to maintain its effectiveness.

Prevent a fire before it starts

All too often, barn fires are caused by carelessness and a lack of attention to potential hazards. A few simple precautions can greatly reduce your risk of fire:

■ *Reduce dust, clutter and cobwebs, especially around electrical outlets, lights and appliances.*

■ *Don't store fuel — gasoline, propane or oil — for farm equipment in the barn.*

■ *Store hay, bedding and farm machinery (tractors, lawn mowers, etc.) in a separate building.*

THE NATIONAL EQUINE SAFETY ASSOCIATION PHOTO

Remove all non-necessary combustibles, including paint, chemicals, fertilizer and pesticides.

■ *Store essential flammable materials (liniments, hoof tars, rubbing alcohol, tack cleaners) behind a fire-proof partition or, in a metal cabinet away from heat sources. Dispose of oily rags in covered metal trash containers. Regularly remove trash; empty grain bags make excellent kindling.*

■ *Keep electrical motors clean. Unplug electrical devices (clippers, box fans, heaters, etc.) when not in use. It's never a good idea to use portable electric or propane heaters in a barn, but if you must do so, be sure to use models with automatic shut-offs in case they get knocked over. Keep them away from hay and bedding.*

■ *Especially in locales vulnerable to wildfires, vigilantly maintain a firebreak around the stable. Clear shrubs, debris and overgrown grass at least 20 feet (50 feet is better) from around the barn, paddocks and storage buildings.*

■ *Absolutely no smoking, no exceptions. Post prominent signs, and insist that violators leave the barn immediately.*

■ *Avoid the use of extension cords. If absolutely necessary, use heavy-duty, industrial-grade, exterior cords, and always unplug them when unsupervised.*

■ *Keep aisleways and exits (your escape routes) clear.*

In a flash of light

According to the NESA, when lightning strikes, nine out of 10 barns will burn to the ground. In one study of 250 equine deaths attributed to lightning strikes, over 40 percent were horses that burned or suffocated in barn fires sparked by lightning.

A properly installed lightning-rod system will harmlessly divert lightning bolts straight to the ground. A standard lightning-rod system, says Bob Winovich, general manager of Western Reserve Lightning Rod Co., includes several 12-inch-tall rods standing a maximum of 20 feet apart along the roof ridge, each connected by a braided aluminum or copper wire running down into 10-foot ground rods. "For instance, if you've got a 70-foot barn, you'd have five rods, one on each end and three spaced out evenly in the middle," he points out. Underwriters Laboratory and National Fire Protection codes specify at least two ground rods for each building, one for every 100 feet of perimeter, and spaced as far apart as possible, such as on diagonal corners.

Winovich estimates that the cost for a 70' x 30' barn would be between $1,000 and $1,500, depending on labor rates. This is not a do-it-yourself project, however. "If a system is installed incorrectly," Winovich cautions, "a lightning strike can cause more damage than if you don't have a system at all."

Of course, lightning rods, alarms and even fire-suppression systems are not the end-all to stopping barn fires. You can't just put in a sprinkler and forget everything else. You must also practice good prevention, says Wilson. "If your whole facility is well-managed, that will reduce the chances that you ever have a fire in the first place." PH

8

Many Levels Of "Clean"

*When it comes to cleaning or disinfecting your barn,
you've got to get the right product for the job!*

E veryone thinks they know what a disinfectant is — something that kills germs, right? In a broad sense, this is correct. However, if the label says "sanitizes" or "sterilizes," is
this the same thing? Are all such products equally effective?
Definitely not.

The labeling of a product as a "disinfectant" does not tell us much.
It could be a sanitizer only or a germicidal. However, even a germicidal disinfectant may not work against all types of germs.

This may sound awfully picky about words and labels, but the fact
is that, in this case, terminology is important. Manufacturers know
that words like "sanitize" catch the customer's attention much better than "clean," although they may mean essentially the same thing.

Also beware of claims such as "anti-xxx" activity or "active against
xxx." These are not claims that a product kills the organisms, and
they provide you with no information as to just how "active or "anti"
they may be. Antibacterial soaps are a good example.

To clean or disinfect

It may sound like disinfecting is always good to do. However, this
is not the case. The environment around us is populated by a teem-
ing, invisible, microscopic world, almost a parallel universe, of
which most of us are unaware. Viruses, bacteria, amoebi and other

such creatures cover every surface, nook and cranny of ourselves, our animals and the environment.

People and animals are protected from harm from these organisms by a combination of natural barriers (the skin and mucus membranes), and the fact that harmless organisms far outnumber the potentially harmful ones.

In a nutshell, the reason that harmless and beneficial bacteria far outnumber the potentially harmful ones is that they have been created to coexist with other forms of life. By sheer numbers alone, the harmless and/or beneficial bacteria in the environment guarantee that the population of harmful forms is kept to a minimum.

While this may sound like an exercise in philosophy, it has a practical application. When you disinfect, you reduce the number of harmful and beneficial bacteria. If this is done too often, the harmful bacteria may gain an edge over the harmless ones when populations begin to reform. Too-frequent disinfection also hinders the ability of the immune system to be prepared for any bacteria that might get past the first line of defense (intact skin and mucus membranes) and gain access to the body, for instance, through a wound.

The horse naturally develops antibodies to the bacteria that are normally present in his regular environment. By constant, low-level exposure through microscopic breaks in the skin or mucus membranes, antibodies develop that make the horse's body better able to quickly and efficiently fight off infection in the event of a more-serious injury.

On the other hand, even usually harmless bacteria can cause problems if their numbers are too high. Bacteria degrade all organic material, including feed residues, and in the process produce substances that are distasteful at best and potentially irritating to the skin or intestinal tract at worst. Some bacteria even produce toxins that can lead to colic or severe illness. The presence of

Chlorine bleach may be used either full strength or in dilution but must be rinsed off.

huge numbers of bacteria also makes it more likely that even minor wounds will become infected.

The answer here is to strike a happy medium when it comes to our neighbors, the micro-organisms. Rule No. 1 — Keep things clean. Note we said clean, not sterile. Routine sweeping, scrubbing, mucking and bathing go a long way toward keeping the numbers of bacteria in the environment at a level that is both safe and beneficial to the good bacteria and to the horse.

On the other hand, in the event of an infectious-disease outbreak, whether bacterial, fungal or viral, you want to call in the big guns. These situations require the use of materials that are "-cidal" to the problem organism.

Defining cleaners

■ *A **disinfectant** is an agent that prevents infection by destroying harmful (pathogenic) micro-organisms. It is almost universally used when referring to products that are applied to inanimate objects, such as walls and floors.*

■ *An **antiseptic** is a substance that kills or prevents the growth of micro-organisms. Iodine is a familiar example. This term is usually used when describing chemicals that are applied to the skin of people or animals.*

■ *A **sanitizer** is a chemical that reduces the number of bacteria present in the environment to a level that is considered "safe." Safe in this instance means a concentration of bacteria that will not normally cause any problems for a healthy human or animal. Soaps and such cleaning preparations as Lysol are sanitizers.*

■ ***Sterilization**, on the other hand, refers to the complete destruction of all micro-organisms by a chemical or physical (i.e. high temperatures) process.*

■ *A **germicidal** agent is a chemical that kills germs — viruses, bacteria, fungi or other types of micro-organisms. Virucidal agents kill viruses; bactericidal chemicals kill bacteria, and so forth. Depending upon the specific product, it may kill bacteria only or also kill other micro-organisms such as fungi and viruses.*

Routine sanitizing

Many common problems, such as wound infections, skin infections, navel ill (infection of the umbilical cord stump) and gastrointestinal problems related to traces of spoiled feed, can be prevented by regular attention to simple cleanliness. In most cases, all you need for these chores is hot water and soap, combined with regular removal of heavily contaminated materials such as manure.

Water buckets and feed tubs should be cleaned daily and thoroughly cleaned every few days (rinsing and wiping out routinely; thorough cleaning with hot soap and water every few days or as needed). If you use sticky feeds or liquid supplements, washing with hot water and soap may be needed daily to ensure there is no build-up of material in the bucket. Not only unappetizing, it also attracts flies, encourages bacterial growth and may reduce feed and/or water intake.

Plastic buckets and feed tubs pose a special problem since they are difficult to rinse free of detergent/soap residue. If the horse is picky, this slight soapy taste may be enough to throw him off his feed or cause a reduction in his water intake. Generally, powdered detergents, such as laundry detergents, are less likely to cause this problem. However, they often do not clean as quickly and easily as "dish soap" products. We have found that Dawn Dish Soap is an excellent choice for buckets, since it cleans well and does not leave a soapy taste.

To remove build-up of feed or manure on the ledges and edges of stalls, without resorting to scrubbing with water or formal cleaning/disinfection, try using the heavy-duty scrubbing pads sold for use on barbecue grills. This will scrape off the material quite well, allowing it to be swept up.

Formal disinfection

If a need for formal disinfection arises, such as with an outbreak of an infectious disease, imminent foaling or after your trailer is borrowed and used by someone else, we recommend this procedure:

1. All movable equipment should be removed, cleaned and disinfected separately. This includes such things as crossties, ropes, ties and mats in trailers, buckets, hay racks, and the like. All feed should be removed, including hay. Ceilings and walls should be swept free of loose dirt and cobwebs. All bedding and organic material (manure) should be raked up and removed.

2. Clean. Scrubbing with stiff brushes and hot soapy water is one alternative, but it is extremely difficult to reach all areas of ceilings and walls with this method. A more-efficient, less time-consuming and actually less-messy approach is to use either high-pressure cleaning or steam cleaning. It is possible to rent high-pressure cleaners that use hot water and detergents, but you will have to shop around a bit. We found one with a day rate of $89 at a rental-store.

Steam cleaning is the most effective approach, but this must be done professionally and rates vary widely. Generally, you can expect to spend several hundred

Anytime an infectious disease is suspected, the animal should be isolated, the barn aisle kept scrupulously clean and a foot bath used outside the stall.

dollars for a professional steam-cleaning job. This is usually reserved for those cases where you are attempting to eliminate a serious infection that survives well in the environment, such as salmonella and many viruses. For more "routine" disinfecting tasks, the pressure cleaners are acceptable.

If you do have an infectious disease problem and require disinfecting, consult with your veterinarian regarding the specific measures to be taken, as these will vary depending on the organism.

3. Disinfect. Sprayers are the most-efficient method of application, either the type that allows you to use premixed solutions or garden hose-type sprayers, where the concentrate is added to a siphon chamber attached to the end of the hose and the desired concentration is set on the chamber. After disinfecting, allow surfaces to dry completely, and air out the premises before returning animals to the barn or using the trailer again. This takes an average of three days, but in times of high humidity can take a week or more, especially if the floors are dirt.

Common disinfectants

SKIN ANTISEPTICS

Preparation: *Iodine solution (2%), iodophores such as Betadine, isopropyl alcohol, hydrogen peroxide, permangenates, silver nitrate.*

Germicidal activity: **High** — *Iodine, iodophores, isopropyl alcohol.* **Relatively low** — *Hydrogen peroxide, permangenates and silver nitrate.*

Comments: *Do not use iodine solutions above 2%. Isopropyl alcohol should be at least 70% solution.*

Toxicity: **Low** *toxicity to skin when used in correct concentrations. Some irritating to mucus membranes (i.e. lips, mouth).* **Moderately to highly** *toxic if ingested.*

ARTICLE/EQUIPMENT DISINFECTANTS

Preparation: *Soaps and detergents, chlorine bleach, Lysol, Pine Sol, isopropyl alcohol, Nolvasan solution, appropriate solutions of concentrated disinfectants (check label first).*

Germicidal activity: **Moderate to high** *when used as directed. Follow instructions carefully regarding duration of time to leave object in contact with the solution.*

Comments: *Washing with regular soaps/detergents and hot water is effective against most pathogenic organisms, especially bacteria. Smooth, non-porous surfaces such as metals (i.e., bits) can be effectively cleaned in this way. Plastics and fabrics may require stronger treatment (check with your veterinarian for guidelines if you are having a particular problem).*

Toxicity: **Moderate to high** *skin toxicity, especially when not diluted, for all agents except routine soaps and detergents.* **Skin chemical "burns" may**

take a few days to appear. Highly irritating to mucus membranes and toxic if ingested. Always rinse well and air dry completely before reusing items.

PREMISE DISINFECTANTS

***Preparation**: There are well over 100 premise disinfectants (for walls, floors, etc.) on the market. Active ingredients include: phenols, substituted phenols, resorcinol, thymo, hexachlorophene, formaldehyde, chlorine, chloramines and sodium, hypochlorite, surface active agents such as benzalkoniumchloride, furan derivatives, sulfurs.*

***Germicidal activity**: **High** — Most premise disinfectants are effective against bacteria, viruses and fungi. However, activity against a specific class of organism or a specific organism within a class may vary.*

***Comments**: If you are having trouble with a specific organism, get the advice of your veterinarian about the product to use. Remove all bedding, hay, grain, feeding and watering buckets, storage bins for grain, supplements, medications, etc. before disinfecting. Follow dilution instructions on the label or from the veterinarian exactly. More concentrated is not necessarily better for disinfecting — only more toxic and more corrosive.*

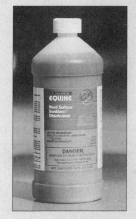

It is often necessary to leave the premises "open" (no animals) for one or more days to allow surfaces to dry and to give disinfectants an adequate time to work.

***Toxicity:** All premise disinfectants are highly toxic. Use protective clothing, goggles, heavy rubber gloves and a mask that will keep out fumes. Discard or launder clothing immediately after disinfecting. Read precautions and first-aid information before you start. Remember, skin absorption and skin damage is also a risk. Avoid all direct contact. Dispose of containers as directed.*

Disinfecting movable objects

When dealing with an infectious disease, it is also important to thoroughly disinfect all objects that have come into contact with either the infected animal or areas potentially contaminated by the infected animal, including yourself! On the human end, hands, shoes and clothing are all potential carriers for infectious organisms.

When a disease is in progress, foot baths should be used outside the sick horse's stall, with feet dipped every time you leave the stall. (Using slip-on rubber boots is almost essential to avoid ruining another type of shoe or boot.) Long-handled brushes should be available at the foot bath to scrub off any adherent dirt, bedding or manure and to allow the disinfectant to get to the surface of the boot.

Another indispensable item is a set of coveralls, which should be put on before entering the stall, taken off when leaving and left hanging in close proximity to the infected area. When removing the coveralls for cleaning, transport them in a plastic bag directly to the laundry area and follow procedures below for blankets.

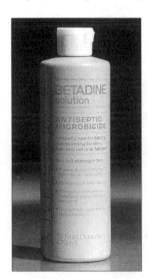

Finally, strict hand-washing procedures must be followed, washing hands after leaving the stalls of sick horses, and also after contact with any of the apparently healthy horses, since it is impossible to tell which of the well animals might actually be infected and not yet showing symptoms.

A surgical-type scrub soap is a good idea for these situations (i.e., Betadine or any povidone-iodine scrub solution). If access to water is a problem, foam hand-cleaning preparations are available that are 62% alcohol; they kill organisms effectively and dry completely without a residue (your veterinarian may have to order these for you).

An alternative is to use gloves. Latex, form-fitting gloves are easy to work with but expensive (even the ones that come in bulk in a box and are not sterilized).

Stall-cleaning equipment used with infected horses should not be used to clean the stalls of other animals. This includes rakes, pitchforks and wheelbarrows. If this is not possible, the sick animal's stall should be cleaned last and equipment disinfected before going back to the stall of a well animal. Wash off all large pieces of debris with soap and hot water. Then soak (10-minute soak) or spray heavily with disinfectant solution and allow to dry (no rinsing).

Buckets, halters and tack used on horses with an infection should be cleaned as above and exposed to disinfectant solution for 10 minutes (fill buckets and soak; soak other equipment). Washing and rinsing after disinfecting is permitted for feed and water buckets and feed troughs only.

Blankets, saddle pads, towels, etc. must also be disinfected. The recommended procedure is to soak them in disinfectant solution for 10 minutes, then launder as usual.

All alcohols are not created equal

Alcohol is a common and effective disinfectant for skin and smooth surfaces. In proper concentration, it can also be used to sterilize instruments.

■ ***Ethyl alcohol*** *(ethanol — the alcohol you can drink) was the first to be used as a disinfectant. It was, and is, very effective. However, ethyl alcohol is also very corrosive.*

■ ***Isopropyl alcohol or "rubbing alcohol."*** *If you intend to use alcohol as a disinfectant, check the label carefully for concentration. Alcohol is sold at a concentration as low as 50%.* *This is fine for wrapping legs and doing massage but is not as effective against organisms. A concentration of at least 70% should be used for disinfecting skin. 90%+ alcohol can be purchased in some drug stores and is the best to buy for disinfection of skin and instruments.*

Choosing a disinfectant

For routine disinfecting of stalls and equipment, when no serious infectious problem is involved, you can use either chlorine bleach, as we'll describe, or Lysol disinfectant solution as described on the bottle. Chlorine bleach may also be used to fight an infection but is easily inactivated by organic material (manure, mucus, etc.) and therefore only really suitable for buckets and small pieces of equipment.

Chlorine bleach in a 1:5 dilution (one part chlorine with five parts water), as recommended on the bottle, is fine for routine disinfecting of walls, buckets and brushes. For activity against viruses, a dilution of 1:3 should be used. Chlorine bleach could also be wiped or sprayed on full strength (i.e., buckets, feed tubs) for quick effect, then rinsed thoroughly with plain, hot water. Movable items cleaned this way should be air dried. In the case of stall cleaning, allow surfaces to dry and the area to air out thoroughly (no strong odor remaining) before putting horses back in.

The active ingredient in chlorine bleach is sodium hypochlorite. The disinfecting effect comes from the chloride it contains. Care should be taken, since this chemical is extremely irritating to the lining of the mouth and nose.

There are hundred of disinfectants on the market. The chemistry behind these substances is quite complicated, and picking the correct solution to tackle the problem at hand is a matter for professionals — your veterinarian and technical staff will be familiar with these chemicals. Again, if you have a serious infectious problem, get professional help before attempting disinfection.

Two widely available disinfectants that are safe to use around horses are Nolvasan disinfectant solution and Roccal-D. You can find these just about anywhere livestock products are sold.

Nolvasan disinfectant solution is manufactured by Fort Dodge and sells for about $35 a gallon. Nolvasan is a trade name that is also used on many other products, such as shampoos and even ointments, although the active ingredient in those products is different from that in the disinfectant. Be sure you get Nolvasan disinfectant, not Nolvasan suspension.

When a virus is of concern, Nolvasan should be diluted three ounces to one gallon of water. For all other purposes, a dilution of one ounce per gallon of water is recommended. The same dilution is used for walls, foot baths and for soaking equipment.

Roccal-D, manufactured by Upjohn, is also readily available in stores or catalogs. The same cleaning procedures are recommended when using this product as with the other disinfectants. Roccal-D is also effective against both bacteria and viruses.

Dilution recommendations are to use four teaspoons (20 cc) per gallon of water for disinfection of surfaces and all hard inanimate objects except for eating and drinking utensils, where a dilution of two teaspoons to one gallon of water is recommended. The price for Roccal-D is about $65 per gallon. However, because you use much less than with many products, it is economical.

Dealing with salmonella

Salmonella is a particularly dangerous, contagious and difficult-to-eliminate bacterial infection that threatens not only your horse but all other living things, including you and your family. Strict isolation procedures must be followed whenever salmonella is suspected.

Disinfection of all areas that have sheltered the infected horse is an absolute must. This is one time when steam cleaning is preferred over plain pressure cleaning as the preliminary cleaning step. Studies have shown, however, that even steam will not completely eliminate this bacterium. Formaldehyde, applied as a fog with the building tightly sealed, is effective in eliminating salmonella from a premises. Formaldehyde is too toxic, however, for use in horse barns.

One recommended procedure is to clean using an anionic detergent (anionic refers to the electrical charge on the surfactant) and disinfect with a phenol-based disinfectant such as Tek-Trol, manufactured by Bio-Tek Industries, Inc.

Toxicity

All disinfectants are potentially highly toxic, especially in the concentrated form. Many people become careless with familiar products and risk injury. For example, undiluted Lysol can cause serious chemical burns to the skin that may not show up until a few days after the exposure.

These chemicals should be stored in their original containers, under a tight seal and in a separate location from commonly used products. When using disinfectants, personal safety measures should be followed. Goggles and a mask (the type that does not allow vapors to enter) should be used. Always wear heavy rubber gloves, protective eye gear and clothing that can be removed immediately after disinfecting tasks are over. Thoroughly rinse all disinfecting equipment before handling it with your bare hands.

Headgear is also advisable, especially if you're disinfecting walls and ceilings and/or using spraying equipment. Regular clothing and as much skin as possible should be completely protected with coveralls. Rubber boots and heavy-duty rubber gloves should complete the outfit.

Most importantly, always follow label directions (or directions from your veterinarian) in preparing the proper dilution of disinfectants. A more-concentrated solution will not necessarily be more effective, but it will be more toxic! ■PH■

9

Covered Options

Wouldn't it be great to be able to ride any time, despite rain, snow or blazing sun? With a covered arena, you can. We'll cover the options, both conventional and creative, for many budgets.

N o way around it, a building big enough to ride in takes a significant financial outlay, especially if you prefer a traditional post-and-beam or all-steel building. But even if you can't afford a conventional structure, you're not necessarily stuck weathering the elements.

Settling on a size

Your first covered-arena decision is determining a size. How much under-roof room do you really need? Consider your year-round training requirements. Do you merely need to cover your 60-foot round pen for rainy-day exercises, or do you want room to practice flying lead changes? Generally, 60' x 120' is a common starter size in traditional buildings. With that much space, you've got room to ride, as well as room to spare. If need be, you can park your horse trailer on one end, or store shavings or hay, or even put up some temporary panel stalls in a pinch.

To set up an under-roof regulation-size dressage arena, however, you'll need an interior minimum of 66' x 132' (20m x 40m) for a small arena or 66' x 197' (20m x 60m) for a large arena. Your actual building, which contractors measure from outside edge to outside edge, will need to be a bit bigger, since support posts along each side take up some inside space. For cutting or reining, arena

Providing shelter from wind and rain, with lots of light, a fabric-covered arena, such as this one by Cover-All, can cost far less than a same-size wood or steel structure.

designers recommend a minimum 80' width, with about 150' or more in length; for jumping, 100' x 200' is better.

Also, consider potential needs down the road — not only your own, but another horseperson's, should you ever decide to sell your property. If you can invest a bit more now to add width or length, you'll make your arena more multipurpose, and your property more attractive in a resale situation. One post-and-beam builder estimated that an extra $5,000 investment now to go from a 60-foot width to a 66-foot width could triple in value 10 years from now.

The bigger-is-better factor also applies to eave height — or, more accurately, the inside height of the truss system's lowest edge. While you may never rope cattle or jump your horse in your covered arena, someone else may want to later (your kids, your boarders, future owners). We've heard horror stories about riders hitting their heads in 12-foot-high arenas, or accidentally roping a truss or light fixture and getting yanked right off the horse. In fact, some top-name barn/arena builders insist on a minimum eave height of 14'; 16' or higher is best for arenas wider than 60'. Team ropers, in fact, often prefer 18' or more because the optical illusion inside (the far end of the building looks shorter) can change the way they throw their ropes, which in turn can affect their outside performance.

Sizing sidenotes

■ *A common rule of thumb for covered or enclosed arenas is that the length should be at least twice the width.*

■ *One popular trend is to build an extra large arena, then line the sides with stalls, combining the arena and barn area under one roof, which is usually less costly than building two separate structures.*

■ *Especially in farming communities, install at least one 24-foot-wide sliding end door (to allow for machine storage, for future resale marketability).*

Where's it gonna go?

Once you know the size you want, you'll have to pick where to put it. Select an area that's easily accessible; remember, you'll have lots of trucks coming in and out during construction. Also consider prevailing winds; if you're planning to leave the sides open, you'll want to catch summer breezes but block winter winds with existing buildings or a line of trees.

Your top priority in site selection, however, is good drainage away from the building. Generally, experts say, you need about one foot of fall (ground slope) for at least the first 10 feet of perimeter.

You'll not only need to divert rain water from running into your arena; you'll also have to contend with rain rushing off of it. The roof of any structure that big can pour a huge amount of water toward your house, into your stables, or out into the paddock. So gutters and downspouts are essential to direct and disperse the water where it won't flood other areas or wash out your driveway. One of the best solutions is to take the water underground to a pond.

Overhead options

Speaking of rain, be sure to include roof insulation in your building plans. Insulation, because of rain? Absolutely. Ever stand under an uninsulated metal roof during a hard rain or, worse yet, in a sleet or hail storm? Imagine trying to ride your horse amid such a racket. A layer of roof insulation will also reduce the likelihood of ceiling condensation raining down on top of you. Ask your contractor to use rigid insulation panels (usually ½" to 1" thick). Avoid plastic-coated foam products or the blown-on type, which birds like to nest in or tear apart and carry away.

Also, don't forget about ventilation. Even with an open-sided covered arena, you'll still want heat, dust and moisture to escape through the roof peak. Some builders recommend ridge vents running the length of the roof; others use cupolas, which are less likely to clog with dust.

What about lights? If you plan to ride only during the day, natural light pouring in through skylights or the open sides of your covered arena may be all you need. Barn/arena skylights are actually opaque fiberglass panels that substitute for standard metal roof panels. Opaque panels disperse the light; clear panels would let in too much radiant heat and create "hotspots" of bright light on the arena floor. Fiberglass panels aren't much more expensive than regular roof panels, but they must be installed correctly so they don't leak.

For night riding, experts recommend installing metal halide lights rather than fluorescent. Although metal halide lights cost a bit more upfront, bulb life and overall energy consumption are better.

Underfoot

If you're planning to use your arena primarily for one specific type of riding or training, consult with professional trainers and/or riders in that field for advice on footing. Some disciplines require soft footing, while others prefer a firmer surface.

For a general all-purpose footing, many arena designers suggest using a specialized footing product, such as ground rubber or processed wood fibers, either alone or mixed with sand, over a clay base. No matter what type of footing you choose, though, you'll probably need to invest in a sprinkler or misting system to keep dust dampened down.

Wood, steel or fabric?

For arenas 72' wide and under, post-and-beam construction is the most common choice. Clear-span wood trusses are available in standard widths of 54', 60', 66' and 72'. Some post-and-beam builders can handle a roof up to 100' wide, but this requires substantially more expensive double-truss systems.

An all-steel structure, such as this one from Heartlight Enterprises, adds lasting value to any property.

Able to span any width you'd want, a steel structure will usually cost more than a similarly sized wood one (up to 72' widths), not only because of the steel itself, but also because of the steel posts' in-ground concrete "anchors." Barring a natural disaster, a steel structure can last forever with minimal maintenance, as long as your contractor uses galvanized steel to retard rust and corrosion.

In some parts of the country, agricultural "quonset" steel buildings are common. With no posts, beams or trusses, quonset buildings are made of huge corrugated-steel arches. The primary problem with quonset buildings (other than rain noise on the uninsulated steel) is that the panels start arching inward from the ground, reducing the inside width for riding. Some companies offer straight-sided styles, where the arches begin at about 8½' high. Quonset styles are typically available up to 100' wide; straight-sided models are 50' to 60' wide or less. Both styles can be disassembled and relocated.

Several companies offer fabric-covered, arched-truss arenas up to 100 feet wide or more (Cover-All Shelter System's Titan structures can span up to 160 feet wide) for usually far less initial cost than a typical post-and-beam or steel building. Some companies even offer monthly-payment lease plans (possibly a good idea before making a big investment, if you're not sure how much you'll actually use an indoor facility).

If you purchase a fabric-covered structure, don't forget to factor in regular replacement costs for the covers, which rarely last as long as a steel-paneled roof (warranties typically offer several-year pro-rated protection). Also, because of the truss-arch design, you'll have to mount the structure on top of a "pony wall," to keep from bumping your head as you pass the truss supports. We're told, however, that the pony walls can be easily constructed by a handy do-it-yourselfer or contracted out locally (if you're all thumbs with a hammer).

In addition to low cost, one advantage of a fabric-covered structure is the sound-dampening quality of the fabric; it's surprisingly quiet inside, even during a rain storm. Translucent fabrics also let in a lot of light; during winter, the fabric can help capture radiant heat to keep the inside warm. Many of the buildings have roll-up sidewalls and roof ridge vents to let in fresh air during summer. Finally, a fabric-covered structure is quite portable — it can go with you if you move.

Covered or enclosed

Ironically, cost doesn't differ much between a covered-only arena and a completely enclosed one, at least in post-and-beam buildings. As Dennis Rusch, with Morton Buildings, explains, "Without outside walls, the roof is more vulnerable to wind gusting underneath it. Once you take off the building's 'skin,' you'll need to spend most of those savings on stiffening the support columns and making the other bracing systems more substantial."

To decide if you still want walls or not, consider your locale's weather extremes. Do you need more protection from winter's bone-numbing wind, or do you need those breezes in the stifling heat of summer? If you need both, consider lining the building's sides with sliding doors, which you can open and close as needed.

Even if you opt for a primarily open-sided arena with roof only, you'll still need a perimeter railing to keep from running into the big support posts. Some people encircle their covered arena with round-pen panels, which they can "borrow," when needed, to build temporary stalls or holding pens. Others build solid walls — of plywood, OSB (oriented strandboard) or even tongue-in-groove lumber — only a few feet high.

"Many people basically just want to get out of the rain and hot sun," says Todd Gralla, of Stan Gralla Architects. "Our pavilion arenas have four-foot or six-foot solid side-walls, and above that, they're totally open. Four-foot roof overhangs keep rain from blowing in, but you still have an airy, naturally lit environment."

Some owners install roll-up or overhead doors for those above-the-sidewall openings. "The nice thing about over-head doors is that you can build them in fiberglass to let in a lot of light," Gralla points out.

If you decide to build an arena fully enclosed with metal panels, be sure to budget for "kick walls" around the inside perimeter of the building, to keep a flying hoof from slicing through (and getting sliced by) the exterior metal. The kick wall can be as fancy a liner as you like, but many people simply use plywood or OSB, both of which can be painted for a nicer finish.

The enclosed (indoor) arena on the top level has sliding windows to allow for air circulation and light. The covered arena below it has round-pen panel walls. Note the drain pipes on both to channel rainwater from the gutters.

Configuring the costs

The cost of your covered arena depends not only on size but also on its type of construction. To cover your 60-foot round pen, expect to spend about $16,000 on a fabric-covered structure from Cover-All Shelter Systems; a "name-brand" post-and beam building could cost between $25,000 and $42,000, depending on amenities (ventilation, insulation, skybelt, etc.). For a 60' x 120' arena, you'll spend about $30,000 for a Cover-All, $42,000 for an all-steel structure from Heartlight Enterprises, $47,000 for a post-and-beam arena by Wick Buildings or $68,500 for a nice post-and-beam arena by Morton Buildings. Any 100' x 200' arena will cost at least $115,000.

Keep in mind that costs can vary widely between various builders/manufacturers. Mr. Local Builderguy may offer to build a structure that costs considerably less than a "name-brand" arena (built by a well-known national or regional contractor), but be sure to ask for — and then carefully compare — written contracts with construction specifications. A company that provides exceptional warranties for wind damage or roof collapse (due to tornadoes or heavy snows) most likely builds for maximum load ratings, using far sturdier materials and construction techniques than the contractor whose bid comes in for lots less. Ask each bidder to explain differences between the estimates — you may find that spending a few extra bucks now may save you major money down the road.

Your own particular circumstances can also affect costs. Contributing factors include your local climate, distance from your chosen contractor and, perhaps, time of year (some contractors offer "off season" discounts). Also remember that prices quoted may not include costs for site preparation, shipping of materials, lights or footings.

Know your local "load" rating

The farther north you are, or the windier your location, the more your arena will cost to build — local codes and permit departments will require your building to meet certain "load ratings," which are based on weather extremes.

Wind load, for instance, indicates the velocity of wind a building must take without blow-down. In many areas of the country, the required wind load is 80 miles per hour.

"Live load," on the other hand, is the amount of snow that a roofing structure can hold. A 40-pound live load means that the roof will support roughly 40 pounds of snow per square foot of roof surface. In Tennessee, a 20-pound live load requirement is common; in parts of Minnesota, it's 80 pounds.

Naturally, the higher the loads, the stronger the roof trussing system must be, which means sturdier — i.e., more expensive — materials spaced closer together (with possibly higher labor costs, as well). In some parts of the country, the seismic zone may mean more support posts.

Round-pen parasols

Certainly, just about any contractor can cover a round-pen-size arena. If your primary goal is simply to shade your round pen from the blazing sun (and if you're pretty handy with tools), your simplest solution may be to put up a "parasol." Sink a few support posts in a square around the pen, construct a quasi-truss system of pipe

With some creativity, one owner has covered a round pen and also provided enough roof overhang for spectators or for room to ride outside the pen.

A benefit of a fabric-covered arena, such as this one from Cover-All, is that you can take it with you if you move.

and/or cable, and then lace sections of tarp-like fabric over and onto the cables. Such fabric, sold in nine-foot-wide sections, is available from KACE International for about $2,500 to cover a 60-foot pen. The company's specialty is a polypropylene fabric cover that wraps around (instead of over) a round pen, to block wind and blowing rain and to help keep footing inside the pen.

If you're particularly thrifty and clever with construction, you can use large tarps (from a discount store, home supply shop or catalog retailer) over a framework of pipe, cable or lumber.

Why not just add on?

To save money, it's tempting to add onto existing structures, where at least one wall is already built. The owners of one horse farm in northern Illinois did just that, hiring a local contractor to add a large enclosed arena to one side of their horse barn. At first, all was fine. Within months, however, rain began to leak along the connection between barn and arena. Today, during heavy downfalls, rain water rushes through the barn aisle.

That's a common problem when trying to add to a standing structure, say experienced barn builders. Multi-roofline connections are difficult to waterproof because seasonal temperature changes cause expansion and contraction, creating cracks and gaps.

For instance, adding two walls and a roof to cover the area formed by an existing L-shaped structure "will be more expensive than if you bought four walls and a new roof of equal square footage," says Morton's Dennis Rusch. "And to add a lean-to to the side of the barn, making a reasonable effort upfront to make it leak-resistant, the cost per square foot will still be higher than if you simply added more length to the end of the structure. The perceived savings of an existing wall isn't enough to pay for the added labor to construct a leak-proof connection."

Making a big box a bit more beautiful

Many covered or enclosed arenas look like industrial warehouses planted in the middle of an otherwise lovely horse farm. Todd Gralla shares the following tips for visually downsizing a behemoth building:

■ *Many arenas look boxy because they're topped by shallow roof pitches (often a flattish 3:12 or even as low as 1:12, which means the roof rises only one inch in height for every 12 inches of lateral width). Increasing the roof pitch to 6:12 can help make the building look more compatible with other farm structures and also enhance inside ventilation, pulling hot air upward and out more readily.*

■ *A hipped roof (one with sloping ends and sides) can reduce the visual scale of the building by breaking up the long expanse of roofline.*

■ *Scissor trusses can help lower the outside walls, bringing the building a little bit closer down to earth. The bottom chord (piece of lumber) of a standard truss goes flat across the "ceiling," parallel with the ground. Scissor trusses, on the other hand, look like the blades of a half-opened pair of scissors — both the top and bottom chords angle upward toward the peak of the roof. So, with a 12-foot eave height at the end of a four-foot overhang, the inside truss height starts at about 13 to 14 feet and goes much higher by the middle of the building.* **PH**

Notes

10

Busting Dust

Not just a nuisance, dust is an early warning sign that your arena footing is wearing out. We'll describe options for fixing your arena before the footing blows away.

W hen it comes to dust, there's good news and there's bad news. First, the bad. There's no perfect answer to eliminating dust, despite the numerous footing and treatment products available. The good news is that we can keep it under control simply by understanding the nature of dust.

Dust and dust dangers

Dust particles — whether originating from sand, wood, rubber or other material — are formed by a disintegration or fracture process, such as grinding, crushing or impact. That fracture process can produce a wide range of particle sizes. Pieces too large to remain airborne settle back down to the ground to await further crushing, while smaller, lighter particles float in the air, to be inhaled by a horse or rider or carried away by the wind.

The key to keeping dust down in your arena is to weigh down those particles by applying something to them or by making sure the footing itself breaks down into particles too heavy to become airborne.

From a respiratory standpoint, dust is Public Enemy #1 for horses. Chronic coughing from dust impedes training and performance. Irritation caused by dust particles can result in permanent respiratory damage.

Using rain birds, you can water an arena quickly, but it requires careful positioning of the nozzle heads to prevent puddles.

In allergy sensitivity tests conducted at the State University of Utrecht, Germany, coughing as an allergic reaction was proven highest in barns with elevated concentrations of airborne dust particles and ammonia gasses.

Unfortunately, physical ailments like respiratory diseases and irritation to the eyes or skin aren't the only hazards (to horses or people). Excessive dust emissions can increase the risk of fire (for instance, think of those flammable, dusty cobwebs); damage equipment (like the barn manager's computer system); impair visibility; carry unpleasant odors; and create problems with local community relations. So you can see why it may be worth spending money and effort on a solution to the dust problem.

The ground war

Sub-Base: The frontline for the war on dust starts at your feet with the sub-base — the arena foundation — built from soil left over after removing top soil and vegetation. You may not have much choice in its composition, but you can make it more impervious to pounding hooves, freezing temperatures and other climactic and environmental effects, which force material above ground where it can be broken down into dust particles.

The U.S. Dressage Federation *Guide to Arena Construction, Under Foot*, advises compacting the sub-base so the soil is as dense as possible. But, don't worry; in soil engineer/construction lingo, "dense" isn't synonymous with "hard." **Density refers to compacting soil to minimize air pockets, pot holes or similar structural gaps.** Your target is a 92 percent maximum density or more (have a soil engineer check the percentage with a density or compaction test before proceeding with a base layer).

The USDF recommends "a large (9- or 10-ton) roller, with or without a vibrator, to compact the soil, because it can apply significantly more pressure than a bulldozer or front-end loader."

Felt and Honeycombs: After compaction, consider geotextiles, or recycled substructure panels for increasing soil stability. These products improve water use and prevent both silt and stones from migrating up from the sub-base. Geotextiles are synthetic, felt-like fabrics sold in varying degrees of thickness (weights) by companies such as ACF West, Inc., and Amoco Fabrics and Fibers.

The geotextile acts as a barrier between the sub-base (and what's below it) and the base/footing above, and helps surface water drain away.

Another sub-structure option is an environmentally friendly, honeycombed grating made from 100% recycled high-density polyethylene, called **Equiground**. Developed at Warendorf — the German Olympic Equestrian Team Headquarters — it provides drainage in bad weather, reducing mud, yet retains water during dry periods, when dust problems increase. Made in 13" x 13" x 1.37" interlocking panels, the grating can be laid without the services of a contractor.

One drawback to geotextile fabrics is that they can tear. Equiground, for instance, is not recommended for turf footings where horses wear caulk shoes, since they can rip up grass and damage the grating — problems that will not occur in arenas using sand, shavings or non-grass footing.

Attack from above

Once you've established the footing, consider a watering or sprinkler system. Commercial watering choices include frost-proof sprinkler systems (excellent for indoor arenas), which hang from the ceiling and produce a fine mist of water. Outdoor, in-ground or landscape-type sprinklers, commonly known as "rain birds," can be installed around the perimeter to cover the full range of the arena.

A misting system is healthy for horses and riders, as it helps remove dust from the air as well as dampen the footing.

Overhead systems offer the best uniform coverage for the least effort, but the downside is that they have to run longer, since water can evaporate on the way down.

Water is transformed into a fine, uniform mist by special nozzles, which are set in the roof of the arena. The dust in the air is weighed down by the mist and carried to the ground, and no puddles or clumps are formed on the ground (as typically found when watering by hand). The system saves time and reduces water use.

For those willing to spend the time, a hand-held hose will do a fine watering — providing you have the discipline and the time. It takes roughly half an hour to water a 10,000-square-foot arena by hand.

Whether opting for a hand-held spray nozzle, movable sprinkler or built-in system, the rule of thumb is to not let any device create puddles or wet spots that can become boggy or compromise the integrity of the arena base. To avoid this with portable sprinklers, move them frequently and check for leaky connections.

Keep dust at your feet

Those tiny, airborne particles that irritate riders' eyes and horses' respiratory tracts are literally shouting, "Danger!" But instead of just cursing their existence, we should realize that dust is a warning that indicates what's underfoot is deteriorating and compromising our horse's safety a little bit more each day.

How much dust you'll have is determined by your choice of footings and footing additives, which run the gamut from natural surface materials to commercially prepared products. Keep in mind that nothing is perfect, but knowing the "personality" of your material will help in choosing its best anti-dust maintenance system.

Sand dust signals that sand is breaking down and needs replacing or is "dirty," meaning it contains clay or other soil particles. *Unwashed sand* is likeliest to have foreign particles. Desirable washed sands are rated as medium to coarse and angulated, including industrial sand (silica) and commercial sands (mason, concrete, beach, number 2).

Avoid *manufactured sand*, which is actually crushed rock that degrades sooner than natural sand. To fix a sand-dust problem, either replace the surface sand or water it regularly, preferably with an absorbing agent.

Coated or *polymer-coated sand* offers minimal dust problems, so long as organic matter that can decompose (manure, leaves, bedding, etc.) is removed regularly. Polymer-coated sand looks and acts like damp sand, whether watered or not. It costs about five times as much as traditional sand footing.

Two commercial examples by Footings Unlimited are *Equation*, a waterproof, polymer-coated sand installed as a three-inch pad over a two-inch cushion, and *Sure Step*, a coarse, granulated plastic that can blend with stone dust or sand at the rate of two to three pounds per square foot. Used outside, Sure Step can approximate an all-weather surface and stay relatively (but not completely) dust-free.

Wood products include shavings, tanbark or bark mulch, sawdust (green or kiln-dried), hogsfuel (a tanbark-type product) and manufactured shredded-wood fibers. Outside, wood footing can be slippery when wet and

Even if you can't afford to use a product like Equiground for the entire arena, installing it in areas where horses congregate, like at the gate, will help minimize dust and mud.

dusty when dry. Shredded wood, unlike shavings or sawdust, decomposes into a topsoil-like material that makes for poor footing. For dust/moisture control, bonding agents help.

Fibar Footing is a commercially-prepared hardwood fiber footing advertised as a low-dust option. For indoor riding, Fibar recommends mixing its product with sand; for outdoor arenas, put a layer of Fibarfelt (the company's own geotextile fabric) down, then add a Fibar/sand mix.

Sand/wood mixes offer the best of both worlds. A good mix uses "green" sawdust or shavings, since the sap content improves moisture levels. Start with 1½ inches of sand to provide traction, then add the wood, which acts as both an absorbing and, to a lesser degree, a bonding agent. Wood's footing life span, since it is an organic material, still won't last more than a year. Even mixed with sand, it will degrade the same way it would if it were the only footing used, so consider fine-tuning the footing with a bonding agent.

Grass or turf produces little dust and is easy to maintain, providing the surface is not overworked. But during droughts, turf gets hard and slippery. Both turf and seeded sod must grow undisturbed for a year to establish deep roots, and you may need soil modification to encourage optimum rooting depth. Without it, turf can divot and tear, kicking up dirt and dust. Geotextiles or similar substructures should never be used with turf, since they restrict rooting depth.

Ground, crumb or shredded rubber is touted by manufacturers as reducing dust because it breaks down slowly, but it also doesn't absorb water, which provides the number one defense against airborne particles. Since rubber is lighter (30 pounds per cubic foot) than soil (80-100 pounds), it can increase overall porosity, allowing water to travel between it and other footing. Lightweight isn't bad for indoor arenas, but rubber used outside can float away in a deluge or blow away in a strong wind.

Used bedding — in hot weather, nothing gets drier, dustier or smellier. Need more be said? But if you must, spread only manure-free used bedding in your arena. The damp bedding will temporarily add moisture to footing, but the resulting ammonia fumes could cause respiratory problems.

PVC (including shredded telephone cable covering) and **shredded leather** are not encouraged as low-dust footing choices. As PVC breaks down, airborne dust can carry harmful chemical fumes, as can "chromed" leather, which undergoes a toxic tanning process.

Synthetic filament mixed with turf or sand artificial fibers (typically made from rubber or plastic) will make for a livelier footing but won't cut dust.

In comparison, the use of **natural fibers**, commercially-produced, like **Fibermate** by Footings Unlimited, can increase moisture and cut dust. Fibermate uses natural coconut fibers extracted from aged husks periodically beaten and hung in the sea for three years to prepare them for final processing. It works best when mixed with dirt or sand and is not meant to be used alone.

Dust + water = more than mud

"But I water my arena!" you say. We're sure you do. And we'll bet it feels like you're out there watering forever. But most people don't run a hose or sprinkler long enough, or let water soak in deeply enough, to do the effort justice. Water needs to penetrate through the top three inches of an arena surface to have any real effect against dust. In reality, most people only dampen the top eighth of an inch.

Your goal is to keep a moisture content of between eight and 12 percent through the top two to three inches of footing or as deep as your horse's hooves go when performing. Using a moisture meter, an inexpensive little tool found in most garden-supply stores, you can determine the moisture content.

Another rule of thumb is to water as deep as you drag. For English riders, that's about one to three inches, two to five inches deep for Western riders. Regular dragging is part of the arena maintenance program that will prolong the life of footing and, naturally, head off problems like dryness and dust.

How much water it will take to reach your optimum moisture content will depend on footing composition, the time of day when you water, and outside forces like humidity and temperature. But it's still the least expensive, most environmentally friendly anti-dust weapon around, as long as two other simple rules are also followed:

■ Water at night so the ground gets soaked without being disturbed by working horses. And cooler evening temperatures reduce evaporation.

> ■ *Water lightly, but often. The trick is not to drown your surface, but water it frequently for short periods, repeating until your meter reads at least eight percent. Once you've established a deep-down dampness, you don't have to resoak as frequently, and if you stay on top of the surface dust (checking once a week) you'll preserve the deep moisture. In very dry weather, or if your ring is on a windy hill (wind is a natural evaporator), you may check it more often.*

Bonding and absorbing agents

A bonding agent holds footing together while increasing its shock-absorbing ability, or "cush," a helpful improvement to any surface where horses are worked. Bonding agents reduce dust by adhering to footing materials, weighing them down and preventing them from blowing away.

Absorbing aids (also considered bonding agents) are synthetic or organically-based substances that absorb and retain water, making dust particles too heavy to become airborne.

Calcium chloride is a white, crystalline compound, commonly known as an ice-melter, which pulls moisture from the air and into footing to combat dustiness. It's easy to purchase, easy to apply, and easy on the wallet (roughly $24 for a 100-pound bag). It's also caustic to the environment, has a drying effect on hooves and, as it evaporates, airborne particles rot tack and corrode metal walls. It's not a good choice.

Broadleaf P4 is easily distributed and works well with slow release fertilizers. Subsequent applications can be reduced by 25 percent to 50 percent.

Environmentally safe oils include food-grade coconut oil, peanut oil, glycerine, lanolin and industrial-grade mink oil. Oil can be expensive, with treatments costing $4,000 or more and reapplications becoming necessary every two to three years.

Used motor oil was once an arena's best friend for reducing dust, but today it is a practice environmentally frowned upon. Industrial waste oil, which contains harmful PCBs, is an even worse choice. Dust coated with these oils will cause respiratory problems and make tack, clothing and equipment hard to clean.

Microbial additives, also known as water additives or organic soil conditioners, are kinder to horses' feet and the environment than calcium chloride. They are applied every time a ring is watered and slow down evaporation (reducing dust) by encouraging the growth of soil-friendly microbes. The microbes also fight dust by producing a natural glue of their own, holding footing particles together and retarding evaporation.

Dust Down, by Footings Unlimited, is a commercial organic soil conditioner. It takes moisture from the air to weigh dust particles down and keep them at ground level, and improves the footing ecosystem.

A weighty issue

No one thing causes dust, and no one thing can cure it. It all depends on such factors as soil PSD (particle size density), percentage of "dirt" or organic matter in a footing, type of wood and its rate of decomposition, amount of watering, grooming/dragging schedules, and climactic influences, like wind, humidity, precipitation and temperature.

To beat dust, weigh it down. Water is the easiest, cheapest and most natural weapon — it's the diligence with which you stick to a watering program that will make the difference. Combining it with the use of an absorbing agent can reduce how often you have to water, but won't free you completely from your responsibilities.

What it boils down to is this: Every surface material ultimately breaks down. Whether or not it turns to dust depends on whether or not it can be prevented from becoming airborne. ■■

Notes

11

Is Vinyl Final?

Described as maintenance-free and impervious to insects and weather, vinyl fencing costs four to six times the price of wood. Is it worth it?

For most of us, the traditional image of horse fencing is the wooden post-and-rail or post-and-board. While more aesthetically pleasing than diamond mesh or non-climb wire — wire fences that are safe for horses — wood fencing is expensive to install and maintain.

One high-tech option advertising beauty, strength, longevity, maintenance ease and safety is PVC (polyvinyl chloride) fencing. When it first appeared in the early 1980s, vinyl fence was criticized for cracking, yellowing and warping. But with advances in technology, the vinyl fence industry has eradicated most of these flaws without sacrificing its advantages.

Fence facts

"If you see a faded vinyl fence, it's probably older than seven years," says Dennis Marcoux of Five-Star Fence, a Heritage Vinyl dealer. "Like most products, vinyl fencing has gone through a learning curve. But in the last five to seven years, it's really come into its own. The bugs have been worked out."

Vinyl fencing definitely offers minimal maintenance — replacing the very rare broken board or post cap and, like with vinyl siding, possibly washing it. But, barring an abnormal happening, vinyl fencing is, as the industry likes to say, "final."

Gardner Fence features two reinforced layers of PVC with a lifetime warranty to the original purchaser.

It's no wonder, then, that the strongest-growing sector of the fencing industry is plastic or vinyl, with a growth rate three times that of other fences. An independent study showed that agricultural users purchased 15.4 percent of all plastic fencing sold, and fence spending, per farm, rose from $156 in 1985 to $243 in 1995.

Why the growth? What's changed? Two major factors: raw vs. recycled plastic, and mono-extrusion vs. co-extrusion production.

In mono-extrusion manufacturing, the fence is made from one "injection," producing a single piece of plastic. Additives, such as UV protection, are found throughout the entire piece.

In co-extrusion, you have two "injections" that flow together and then form one piece. The UV-protection additives are only in the outer surface, with the theory that that's the only place they are necessary. Co-extruded fence is less expensive to produce.

Co-extrusion may use varying grades of material in its inner and outer layers, possibly including the company's own regrind and/or recycled materials. Once it's produced, however, you can't separate the layers, which are bonded together. If the right materials and additives are used, the fence works well.

"Co-extruded PVC is similar to veneer furniture," explains Gigi Fletcher of Saratoga Fence and Rail, a maker of mono-extruded fence. "The difference between the two is not as important as it used to be. Most co-extruded manufacturers make good products." However, some do not. There's probably a good reason why the vinyl "horse fence" at your local home-improvement supply house sells for what seems to be an incredible deal. Buyer beware: The warranty that comes with the fence is more important than what the fence looks like before you put it up. The warranty is likely an indication of what quality materials are used in the processing.

"PVC is like a cake recipe," comments Sharon Fullen, with Royal Crown Fencing, makers of Triple Crown Fence. "It's only as good as its ingredients." ASTM (American Society for Testing and Materials) standards allow the use of recycled plastic (known as "grayback") for the core, but not the exterior, of vinyl fencing. And a company is allowed to use only its own regrind; using recycled fence from another company's manufacturing waste doesn't meet ASTM standards."Adding waste, or regrind material, isn't necessarily a bad thing," says Fullen. "But it adds an unknown element to the product."

BUYER BEWARE:

THE WARRANTY THAT COMES WITH
THE FENCE IS MORE IMPORTANT THAN
WHAT THE FENCE LOOKS LIKE BEFORE
YOU PUT IT UP.

Mono-extrusion fans claim it offers greater strength. However, the changes that have been made in co-extrusion processing are making that point less definitive. Although vinyl fencing is unlikely to splinter even under impact from a charging horse, it is a remote possibility. "If the temperature dips below zero — and a horse hits it hard enough — it might crack from the stress," says PeeWee Baker of Penrod Fence Construction. But it won't crack just because it's below zero — that problem's been eliminated in the manufacturing process. Even rocks thrown at it from a nearby lawn mower are unlikely to cause a crack. "A rock might leave a dent, but the board is reinforced and denser than vinyl house siding, so it's probably not going to break." The belief that co-extruded fence is similar to particle board is simply incorrect.

Almost maintenance-free, Centaur fencing looks like traditional board fence from a distance.

Centaur Fence

Centaur Fence offers an interesting alternative to rigid vinyl fences. Centaur fence is made of high-tensile wires covered with mono-extruded polymer. It's not a true wood look-alike, since it's not as thick as rigid vinyl but from a distance it may be difficult to recognize the difference. Centaur fence is a copolymer plastic with wires imbedded inside, offering the low-maintenance of vinyl fencing with the flexibility of wire.

Centaur fence offers more flexibility than rigid vinyl because it literally comes in long rolls and is hung on the fence posts through brackets. You don't nail the Centaur fence to the post; you attach the brackets to the post and run the fence through them. This allows the fence to slide through the brackets, like a belt through belt loops. Centaur's patented bracket system makes this a true "continuous run" fence.

Centaur provides an 84-page step-by-step, well-illustrated manual for installation. Properly installed, this fence may require rare tightening of the wires, says representative Molly Wood, but otherwise should be trouble-free.

Consumer advice

Since all PVC fence is not created equal, we sought the advice of experts for a few smart consumer tips.

■ **Tensile PSI**: This refers to the ASTM test for determining the tensile (greatest longitudinal stress a substance can bear without tearing apart) properties of plastic. A specimen is subjected to temperature, humidity, pretreatment and speed tests; the result is specified in PSI (pounds per square inch). The higher the PSI, the greater the tensile strength or, in layman's terms, the greater the overall strength and durability.

■ **Horse "Wear"**: Obviously, horses are hard on fencing-rubbing on it, leaning over it and sometimes chewing on it. Is vinyl horse-proof?

Chuck Buchholz of Country Estate says, "The fence is designed so the rails will come out without damage to the animal. Depending on where the horse hits, there may be damage to the posts or rails." But this damage isn't likely to be chips or dangerous slivers. Electric stand-off wires can be set on the inside of the fence to keep horses from rubbing on the fence or trying to lean over it.

"I recommend electric wires with any vinyl fence used for animals," said Karen Mockensturm of Ramm Fence. "If you have a horse who rubs on the fence a lot, there is a chance he can rub a rail out."

"Money is a factor, of course," continues Fletcher. "If you have stallions, for instance, you might want to run two aisles of fence between paddocks."

Chewing is unlikely to be a problem with vinyl fencing. It's just not satisfying to the chewer, as it's slick and doesn't splinter like wood. If your horse does decide to "taste" the fence, chances are he won't harm it. "It depends on the horse's teeth and bite, of course. The fence is so hard and stiff, it deters them from chewing," says Baker. If the horse bites hard enough, he may leave tooth marks, but it's unlikely he'll hurt the fence or himself, or make a habit of it.

■ **Pricing**: "In general, vinyl fencing costs between $2 and $6 per linear foot," notes Fullen. "Variances between companies are small, and depending on conditions, you can pay as much for low-grade PVC as top-quality." Her first suggestion is to buy in volume to take advantage of reductions for buying quantity and to limit expensive shipping costs. Vinyl pays for itself in only five to seven years. Local pricing, she advises, may also be lower than a company's general

Rigid vinyl fencing such as Ultra Guard's, has the look of traditional post-and-rail fencing.

quote, so plan your fence project well ahead to have time to check market fluctuations.

According to calculations by Gardner Fence System of Minneapolis, the cost of erecting and maintaining a wood fence on 2½-acres overtakes the expense of vinyl fencing in the seventh year. Over 20 years, the total cost of vinyl fence remains at its initial installation (approximately $6/ft or $7,920) compared to the cost of painting, staining and replacing wooden boards ($14.50 to $17/ft. or $19,140 to $22,440).

■ *Color*: Choose white over dark or black rails. Dark colors may streak or fade, and sun may makes them brittle. Some manufacturers even have a different warranty for colored rails, so look at the fine print.

Vinyl fencing is also not impervious to the effects of chemical fertilizers or rust in a water system. Both damage color, but not structural integrity. "Don't try to paint over a stain," says Fullen, "because the paint won't stick. Just eject the rail and replace it."

Chuck Buchholz of Country Estate says the company president has had the same vinyl fence for 30 years, and it "maintains its characteristics." If anything, he says, it's actually become whiter, due to the chemicals in the vinyl to maintain UV protection.

PeeWee Baker of Penrod Fence Construction agrees: "Bleaching and similar problems depend on the brand of fence. In our products, 96 to 97 percent of the material is natural, which makes it less likely to have problems."

■ *Maintenance*: The main maintenance factor of vinyl fencing is washing. In some parts of the country, you can get mold and mildew on the fence if it's wet enough. You might use a combination of bleach and water or vinyl-siding wash to clean your fences. A high-pressure washer can be a big help, but otherwise the old bucket and sponge will get the job done. Check with your fence manufacturer for specific instructions on the best methods and washing solutions for your fence. However, if the dirt and mud don't bother you, that's fine, too. It doesn't affect its structure.

■ *Warranty*: The best way a company can demonstrate confidence in its product is through a written warranty, so ask for one. Also, since it's difficult for the consumer to tell the difference between PVC products, identify the vinyl manufacturer and not just the supplier or dealer. The best manufacturers want you to buy through their authorized dealers so they can stand behind their product. Less scrupulous sales methods can lead a consumer to believe that a vinyl fence is actually "made" by a certain outlet, when in fact the outlet is only a supplier or dealer.

Warranties can differ not only in length, but in responsibility, depending on whether they're written through the manufacturer or dealer. And with a lifetime warranty, check to see if it covers everything, or just certain situations and parts.

Ask how long they've been selling the product, and how long they've been in business. You're more apt to have confidence in a lifetime warranty from a company that's been around for a while.

■ *Installation*: Most fencing professionals will tell you that a fence is only as good as its posts. Set your posts following manufacturers' directions to the letter. If you have a question during installation, call for advice.

Gates

Consider the convenient location, adequate width and proper installation of your gates. An important part of your fencing, gates can be an annoyance or hazard if they're the wrong size or don't swing conveniently.

We prefer horse gates that swing both ways freely, which is simply a matter of properly setting the hinge on the post. Otherwise, your main consideration is which side of the fence the post will sit. This is mainly a matter of preference, but if you're unsure talk with your contractor. A good fencing professional should be able to offer advice on position and gate location specific to your barnyard set up.

Electric stand-off wires can be used to keep horses from rubbing on the fences.

For width, check the size of your current and future equipment. If you're dreaming of a 15-foot bushhog to mow the fields, don't put up a 12-foot gate. And don't forget your horse's hips. Even if you don't have heavy equipment to bring in and out of your gate, you don't want it so narrow that your horse will scrape his side when he goes through it. Five feet is a likely minimum safe width for a field gate.

Remember that the longer the gate, the more trouble you'll have with sagging. (While double gates are an often suggested option, we generally find them awkward to use, and they can be dangerous when taking one horse out of a field with other horses in it.) While there are braces and gate wheels that can help control sagging, the most important part of your gate is the post.

Gate posts should be bigger than your regular fence post and set in concrete to help support the gate. If the gate's weight causes the post to shift in the soil, your gate is more likely to sag and not open properly. You may also opt for supporting it with steel tubing inside the vinyl fence post.

Wood vs. PVC

Wood
- *Decay or rot common.*
- *Pressure-treated wood may contain arsenic, creosote, carcinogenic heavy metals or lead-based paint.*
- *Splinters, weakens, exposes rusty nails.*
- *Spooked horses can get hurt on impact. Rails may cut or impale a horse, as fence breaks or splits.*
- *Encourages chewing or cribbing.*

PVC
- *Never rots.*
- *Only nontoxic materials used.*
- *Sliver-proof; nails not a danger, nor sharp edges.*
- *Flexes on impact. Less likely to splinter or cut.*
- *Smooth surface difficult to grip.*

The bottom line

Ask specific questions about the warranty. Does it cover normal horse wear? (Probably not; ask them to define it.) Find out about availability of replacement parts. While "vinyl may be final," accidents do happen. If your tractor driver accidentally turns left instead of right and drives through your fence, you're going to need repair parts quickly.

Bear in mind location and shipping costs when choosing a fence company. Sometimes a local dealer who seems to have "higher" prices will be able to match or beat a distributor who has to charge higher shipping fees.

When choosing your vinyl fence brand, consider the location of the dealer. If you must have the material shipped 1,000 miles vs. 20 miles, you're going to eat up any material savings in added shipping costs. Compare costs among dealers in your area. And don't be afraid to ask for the "best price" a company can give you. ▣

Notes

12

Electric Fence Savvy

Electric fence is both cheaper and more mobile than other kinds of fencing. With care, and understanding of its limitations, it can be just as safe — or safer — than conventional fencing.

id you ever wish you could try out a new internal fence configuration without the effort and cost of sinking posts and nailing rails? Want to limit your horses' access to spring grass while still letting them out to pasture all day? Do you need to keep horses out of the mud beside the barn during spring runoff times, or keep them off a newly seeded area? If so, then electric fence may be just what you need.

Limitations

The very nature of electric fence gives it some limitations. It may be harder to see than other types of fencing, and its temporary status makes it subject to the surprise factor ("it wasn't there the last time I ran across this field"). Used alone, it will not absolutely contain horses — it can be broken or knocked down, and a horse moving fast enough will merely get shocked as he breaks through it. Don't rely on electric fence alone to keep horses on your property or off roads, or to keep your neighbor's animals out. Traditional perimeter fencing is necessary for your horses' safety, and you can be held legally liable for injuries and damage caused by your horses if they run free. Some other considerations before using electric fencing alone:

■ Don't use electric fence to separate mares and foals from each other, or to separate stallions and mares.

■ Don't use it if your horse hasn't been trained to respect the fence.

■ Don't use it where horses run and play, for example, in a turnout area for horses who normally live in stalls.

■ Don't tempt the horses with a strong reason to get to the other side. When their buddies are running and playing, or when the grass is too tempting on the other side, even the best behaved horses may challenge the fence. When rotating sections of pasture, change the fence location before the grass runs out.

■ Don't use electric fence to fence a small area with a relatively large number of horses; horses lower on the pecking order are likely to get pushed into (or through) the fence.

Electric fence is also not a good idea for areas where the public is likely to come up against it. On any type of electric fence, in any location, it is a good idea to post signs. Be sure to supervise toddlers and keep them away from electric fences.

Weather that doesn't affect traditional fencing can decrease the effectiveness of electric fence. Ice on electric tape or wires can weight them down to the ground.

AFTER YOU'VE SET IT UP,

TAKE THE OPPORTUNITY TO STAND BACK

AND LOOK AT THE FENCE — IF THERE IS

ANY QUESTION OF VISIBILITY,

TURN IT OFF AND FLAG IT WELL.

Fence posts

Both permanent and temporary posts of varying stabilities are available. You may choose all temporary posts for your fence, or you may find that the fence ends or corners require stronger posts to handle the tension on them from the fence itself. Some temporary posts may be pushed into the ground by hand, particularly if the ground is soft. Others have a foot rest and can be pressed in that way. Metal T posts can be put into most any type of ground with the help of a manual post driver.

If the idea of metal posts brings visions of impaled horses, you can purchase caps that also act as electric fence insulators, or get your tennis-playing friends to give you their old balls. A sharp knife will allow you to slice an opening just large enough to fit the tennis ball down onto the top of the post. For even more stable and permanent posts, you may need a post-hole digger (manual or tractor-driven), wooden posts and possibly even concrete. The strongest corners and end-post configurations are those shaped like an H, with a pair of posts, connecting wires, and a sturdy cross piece.

Electric wire can stop horses from leaning on a nonclimb horse fence.

Whether you choose permanent or temporary posts for your corners, angling them slightly (an inch or more) away from the center of the enclosure will help keep the stretched fencing from pulling them in. For temporary applications, one or two additional posts, set so they lean against the corner post from the inside, can be added to reinforce the corner post against fence pressure.

Curves generally work better than corners to keep the entire fence line upright because there is less tendency for the posts to be pulled in. When changing the direction of the fence line in a rotational grazing section, or building a holding area for horses on an overnight pack trip, we recommend curving the line or making an oval enclosure.

Standard fencing requires anywhere from 8' to 12' between posts. Electric fencing is much more versatile, with as much as 30' to 40' between posts. The terrain, grass height and stretch of the fence will determine how far apart your posts can be set. Because the electricity will ground out (go into the soil rather than along the fence) when the fence wire touches high grass, you will need to gauge the post distance so that the slight looping inevitable with temporary hand-strung fencing won't bring the fence into contact with the grass.

When dealing with high grass or bushes, you can mow or weed-eat under your fence line to both avoid shorts and the horses' temptation to graze underneath it. When moving fence lines during rotational grazing, keep the fence slightly inside the previously grazed section with its short grasses.

Location

To avoid accidental run-throughs that wreak havoc with your stay-away-from-the-electric-fence training program, think, and look at the fence like a horse when setting up the fence line. Avoid stringing the fence where horses will come upon it suddenly and see it too late — like around the corner of the barn or in a thicket or a tree line. Avoid stringing it across their normal path. Even with these precautions, you should lead your horses around a newly fenced area so they have the opportunity to see the new fence location before being turned loose. Once the horses get used to the fence changing locations, they will look for it.

Fence materials attached

Electric tape attached to wooden fence posts can provide a traditional look.

When dealing with electric fencing, the height of the single, or top, wire on the posts is a function of the terrain, grass height and your horses. Traditional fencing averages 4½' high, but electric fencing can be much lower. If you are running one electric wire (or tape or rope), generally, chest high to the horses works the best; higher than that encourages them to reach farther underneath, while lower begs them to reach over.

If you are running multiple wires, you can raise the top one and add those underneath at appropriate spacing. Be sure the lowest wire is not so low it gets shorted out on the grass. On uneven terrain, the fencing can be connected at different heights on the posts to make an effective barrier.

While the tendency of horses to lean and push on traditional fencing dictates that traditional fence material be attached inside the posts, electric fence wire can be strung inside or outside. When you have a choice, string the fence inside the posts. For curves or corners, wire strung outside the posts puts the pressure on the posts instead of the insulators.

Visibility

Visibility is always a concern with electric fencing. The single-wire, braided/poly wire and ropes can be difficult or impossible to see when the sun is in your eyes, against snow or in low light. Even electric tape can be difficult to see in some circumstances.

The simplest method of improving summer visibility is to tie strips torn from an old bed sheet to the wire. These can stay on the fence when it is rolled and unrolled at a new location, and are lightweight even when wet. You can also purchase plastic tape for flagging, which comes in a variety of colors (some that will be more visible in snow). Clip-on plastic fence flags won't slip along the fence when the wind blows like rags do, but they get in the way when rolling up the fence and are more expensive. For winter use, choose dark-colored fencing and flagging materials.

Electrical concerns

One of the beauties of electric fencing is that it does not have to form a loop back to the point of origin. It can be strung in a line, keeping in mind that the end of the line must be attached in a visually imposing, but non-conductive, barrier to the perimeter fence, building, etc. It can be run from the charger at one side of the gate, around the paddock, and to the other side of the gate without the need to electrify the gate and with no loss of power. If your gate does not need to be electrified, this is ideal.

If you need to run electricity underground, for example, under a conventional gate, you can run the wire in a buried 1/2" PVC pipe. Or, you can purchase wire that is designed to be buried without leaking current into the ground.

An insulated gate handle attached to electric fencing allows you to have a temporary, low-cost gate. Plan ahead for gates when setting up the fence. If your fence does not attach back to itself at the charger, you can make the open gate not electrified for ease of handling. For this, have the charger on the side of the gate where it

latches. If you have a continuous loop of fence, or if the charger is on the gate hinge side, the gate will be electrified and must be handled with care. If you get shocked, the current can pass through your lead rope and also shock the horse you are leading.

The strength of chargers varies according to the length of fence you want to charge and whether you need to shock through high grass or not. We've found that the longer the fence the harder it is to keep it from grounding out at some point, but you can minimize this problem by buying a charger

This fence charger takes six ordinary D-cell batteries.

designed for the distance you plan to cover. Some electric-fencing manufacturers specify the type of charger to use (often a low-impedance type that won't burn the wires); be sure the charger is appropriate to the type of fencing you are using.

The fence charger will have three ports: one to the fence, one to the source of power and one to the "ground," literally a rod in the soil. The ground is necessary to complete the circuit. That's why birds can light on electrified wires and not get shocked — the current does not travel through them. With horses and people, the current travels from the fence through our bodies (hence the shock) and to the soil below. The current travels in the soil to the ground rod and completes the circuit.

Testing the fence

Once you've set up your fence, you'll want to test it to make sure the charge is coming through. Our simplest field test is to hold a blade of green grass in our finger tips and touch it to the fence — we can feel the pulse but normally won't get shocked. If you are playing it safe, or want a more accurate test, you can purchase a fence tester. Place the tester's ground probe into the soil, extend the wire so the unit touches the fence, and it will give you a visual readout of the fence current strength. The expensive models tell you more specifically how much current you have; we find that it's enough to know that the current is running reasonably well.

Moving the fence

We've mentioned that one big advantage of electric fencing is that it is relatively easy to move. One method is to roll up the fence as you walk along. The fence can then be stored on the spool, or unrolled onto newly located posts. This works best for woven-wire and narrow-tape. Plain wire must be handled this way to avoid kinks that weaken the wire, although you will find kinks as you roll even if you're careful. The wider webbing requires a bigger spool that gets heavy quickly. You might be able to use the spool that the fence material came on. If you are inventive, you can add handles that make it much easier to roll it as you walk.

The roll-as-you-go fence-moving technique can be done by one person, but it's easier with two. One can disconnect the fence from the posts while the other person rolls.

There will be times when you are rotating the horses to the next nearby section of your large pasture. In this case, you have two lines of fence with the horses grazing between them. You only need to move one length of fence and can leap-frog it over the other length to give the horses access to a new ungrazed section.

When moving a whole section of electric fence, the easiest method is to disconnect it from the posts and have a number of people carry/drag it across to its new location. This eliminates the time spent rolling and unrolling, but requires many helpful hands to keep from kinking the fence or getting it snagged on the ground.

Other animals

Be aware that other animals have different fencing needs than horses. Cows will press fence capacities more than horses, so a substantial shock and heavy fencing is desirable for them. They don't panic like horses do when caught, so plain wire can work well. Goats and sheep need fence wires closer together and closer to the ground.

Wildlife nearby will influence your fence choices, too. Deer and elk move so quickly that they may not see a thin electric fence and may break it, leaving an escape route for your horses. If deer and elk are common, choose highly visible horse-type fencing.

Adding the horses

Training horses to respect an electric fence is easy — it just takes time and attention on your part. Preparing a training area can give you practice setting up shorter lengths of fencing before you enclose a larger area.

Set up a length of fence within a familiar area that already has a perimeter fence. Choose a holding-type area where the horses can approach and retreat from the fence rather than a place where they are used to moving through.

A round pen is smaller than ideal, particularly for a horse who is flighty, but will do in a pinch for a more staid individual. You want an area small enough that the horses can't ignore the fence, yet big enough that they can actually run away (you want to encourage them to stay away from the fence).

Electric fencing can be used as a temporary holding area away from home — for overnight camping next to your trailer at a competition or to contain your horses on a pack trip.

Introducing them to the fence

Expect that the first time they get shocked, the horses might turn and run for some distance to get away. Placing your training fence within a yard of the perimeter fence will encourage the horses to bolt away from (not through) the electric fence. Choose a place with good footing; you don't want them sliding into the fence, or slipping and falling as they run away. You can set up the fence to go along the length of one side of your enclosure; it does not have to be a complete loop. You don't want the horses to be able to get around behind it and get trapped; this may force them to run though it in order to get away, and that's not what you want to teach.

When you connect the electric fence to your existing fence, be sure it does not short out the electric fence. A short length of non-conductive material will attach your electric-fence post to your existing fence.

People will tell you that you don't have to have the fence on all the time; that the horses will think it's on. In our experience, many horses quickly learn to associate the clicking sound with the charge and can tell the difference. Certainly, during training times you want the fence on all the time.

After you've set it up, stand back and look at the fence — if there is any question of visibility, turn it off and flag it well. When all is ready, turn the horses loose and observe them from a distance. You don't need to be right there. In fact, since you want them to respect it when you're not around, you may as well be out of sight. You don't want to betray their trust by having them come up to you and get shocked by the fence, so don't tempt them or lead them up to it.

Beyond the introduction

If the horses have not tested it, they may not have learned about it. It only takes one shock for most horses to learn. Horses will watch each other and hence avoid it when their buddies do, but consider if they are there alone — they still need to learn as individuals. This may take hours — plan to spend enough time watching to be sure they have all learned their lesson. It's a good idea to leave the fence up in their paddock for a few days for reinforcement purposes, and you can do the same at the beginning of the season if you use it only cyclically.

You may need to add incentive to get them to touch it if they ignore or stay away from it at first. We believe that it is safest for them to be shocked, first, when in a controlled situation — you don't want them to experience this for the first time in the middle of their pasture where they might bolt through the fence. Be aware that wet ground will facilitate the circuit completion — the shock — so if you have sensitive or particularly flighty horses, dry ground might be a better choice for training. PH

13

Electric Fence Selection

*Electric fencing can give your operation flexibility,
but when it comes to choosing products,
the options are overwhelming.*

lectric fencing has traditionally been used to keep wildlife
out and cattle in, but horse-friendly electric fence is a relatively new addition to the market. When determining
what is right for your operation, be sure to request catalogs from manufacturers of the products that you are considering
and talk with other horse people about their experiences. We'll
give you the lowdown on selecting the right components for electric fencing.

Conductors: fence materials

To simplify, there are five choices in electric-fence material: wire,
wire twisted or braided with plastic, wire braided through rope,
wires laced through plastic tape, and electrified PVC boards.

Electric wire is the cheapest conductor and is therefore useful
when stringing miles of fencing in huge pastures where the horses
won't get pushed up against the fence. It is an ideal — probably the
best — electrical conductor because it will carry a charge over miles
of fence.

It can be used as a single strand, although its visibility is poor. A
better use is as the lower wire on a fence with a highly visible tape
on the top. If used alone, it is absolutely necessary to flag the wire
for visibility.

Because aluminum or steel wire is fairly thin, it might break if a horse gets caught in it (but probably not until it does some damage). It is relatively difficult to handle as it tends to kink and then break. Splicing is easy, but it requires a wrap rather than a loop or knot to avoid kinks. This fence is inexpensive and it will last a fair time, but we prefer other types.

Wire twisted or braided with a plastic-type material is one step up from plain wire. Though more expensive, it has advantages. Price is based on the variation in the number of wires twisted together and the plastic material, which varies in strength and visibility. For the most part, the more expensive products have stronger plastics and better conducting wires (either more wires or more conductive alloys).

Twisted wire is extremely easy to handle; it rolls and unrolls easily, doesn't kink or break, and is lightweight. It is easy to splice — just untwist, gather and twist the wires, and knot the plastic for strength.

Visibility is better than with plain wire, particularly if you choose plastics in two contrasting colors. The lighter color shows up against dirt, grass, foliage and night sky, while the darker color

An electric wire or electric tape is often used to discourage horses from chewing wood fencing or from playing across the fence

shows up against rock, dust, snow and stubble. We still recommend flagging it.

Twisted wire can be used alone with better results than plain wire, or it can be used for lower wires under a more visible tape. While it will break if a horse hits it hard, it can still cause injury. Its useful life is nearly as long as that of rope, even if rolled and unrolled many times. We recommend it if it fits your operation.

Ropes with wires braided through them are more expensive still and are similar in price to the wider tapes. They are stronger than the twisted wires and less likely to slice a horse, but they also are less likely to break if a horse gets tangled in them. They carry a charge reasonably well, although this depends on the wire used. They roll and unroll easily, but a roll gets heavy quickly, particularly if wet. The fence posts and insulators must be stronger than with the plain wire fences to handle the weight of the fence, and you need to factor in the added weight of rain and ice.

Visibility also depends on the colors, and we recommend two-color products. Being thicker than twisted wire, the wire has better visibility, but flagging new areas of fence is still recommended. The psychological barrier of rope is somewhat stronger than that of wires, but even the manufacturers warn against electric rope that resembles anything used in riding or training our horses. Splicing is done with metal connectors that add slightly to the cost. We recommend ropes if they meet your operation's needs.

Plastic tape with wire varies from ½ to 1½ inches wide; prices increase with width. Tapes carry a charge reasonably well. They are not as easy to roll as twisted wire, tendening to twist, and will last longer if they are not sharply bent in rolling. Wider tapes are heavier to roll and carry but are more visible. Splicing can be tedious; the best connections are lengths of bare wire knotted to lengths of bare wire with the plastic fibers also knotted for strength.

Wider tapes will blow in the wind. That added tension requires a stronger connection to the posts (or shorter distance between posts). Ice will weigh the tapes down, potentially to the ground. Expected life approaches that of electric rope. While the wider tapes, particularly, are unlikely to break if a horse gets tangled, they are softer than many other fencing materials. Tapes are recommended.

Electrified PVC board fence is many times more expensive than the other options, but it is nearly the equivalent of a permanent board fence. It has the psychological barrier effect of a board fence, looks smooth and even enough for your front yard, is durable, and has the electricity to keep horses from leaning, rubbing or cribbing. Any lack of strength compared to board fencing is made up for by

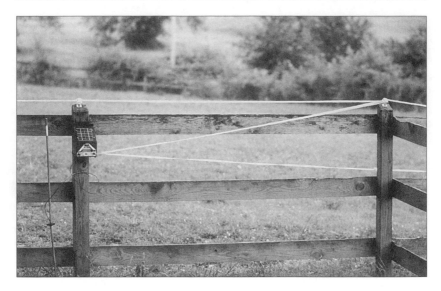

The trick to using a solar charger effectively is to put it in a sunny location and out of reach of the horses. This charger is powering an electric tape on both the top and middle boards to prevent cribbing.

the decreased pressure of horses avoiding the electric charge. The eight-foot PVC boards have two (electrified) aluminum rails running the length of the inside of the board and are designed to be installed as a three-board fence. If you choose, you can substitute non-electrified boards for the lower rails. The posts can be wood, metal T posts (with or without PVC covers), or 4" x 4" PVC posts. Unlike wood fences, no painting is required.

While the manufacturer provides straightforward instructions, this is permanent fence construction, and the evenness and attractiveness of your results will reflect your time and effort. If you find this type of fence attractive, it's only real down side is cost.

Posts

Traditional wood posts or metal T posts can be used for electric fencing. PVC sleeves for metal T posts can be purchased to dress up your fence. Fiberglass posts include step-in base posts with metal stakes, built-in insulators, and smooth pencil-pointed rods that accommodate a variety of insulators.

End posts

If your conductor is lightweight, and you move your fence frequently, you can get by with simple straight fiberglass posts for end posts. Some users plant two or three and tie them together at the top to make a more secure brace. Fiberglass posts are the cheapest and lightest in weight, but they are not as stable as other posts. Uncoated fiberglass can splinter, so gloves are in order when handling it — or you can buy the more expensive coated fiberglass rods.

Metal T posts or wood posts make more stable end posts. These allow you to keep enough tension on the fence wire to keep it from sagging. Even if your fence does not attach to these end posts all the time (if you rotate your fencing or use it seasonally), it is well worth your time to sink strong posts for the ends of your wires.

Line posts

Plastic handles help you open and close the "gate," and extra poly/wire can be stored on the fence itself.

Electric fence line posts don't have to be anchored as strongly as end posts, and they can be spaced farther apart than traditional fence-line posts. They don't need to hold up to much tension, as their function is mainly to keep the wires off the ground and correctly spaced (if you are using multiple wires). The terrain, weather, height of the grass and the components you choose all determine how far apart you can space your posts. Use the manufacturer's suggestions as a starting point and go from there. While you don't have to space posts closely, remember that they contribute to the fence's visibility, so in training stages or new locations, extra posts can be an advantage.

Connectors

Electric rope and the thicker tapes are best connected with manufactured connectors. The rope connectors look like cable splicers, and tape connectors look like buckles. Plain wire is easy to connect with a special knot. Braided wire and the small tape can be unraveled, the wires twisted together, and the plastic fibers knotted together for strength.

Connectors or hand-made connections are not only useful for joining the ends of two rolls, they are useful in case of breakage and for when you had previously cut the fence material for a shorter application. While extra unused fencing material can be hung on its reel from the last fence post (as long as it is secured away from other wires and up off the ground), there are times when this is not convenient and we find we have to cut the conductor.

Connectors of a different kind are needed to link the different conductors in your fence if you've strung more than one strand of electric fence. These connectors are usually insulated wires with clips on both ends.

Tensioners

These connect to end posts and are used to take up the slack in fencing materials. They may or may not be necessary, depending on your operation, and are specific to the conductor you use. With fiberglass posts and low-tension twisted-wire or tape fencing, you can adjust the tension adequately by taking a few more wraps around a fence post.

Insulators and extenders

There are more types of insulators than there are types of conductors. The insulator must fit the conductor and match the post. We recommend you choose your conductor and type of post, then shop for insulators based on both an appropriate fit and function. Some insulators are designed for corners, others for straight-line fence. Insulators are available that connect two or three wires. Some insulators allow the conductor to slide through, while others anchor the conductor. Normally, anchoring insulators are used on end posts, and the line posts allow the fence material to pass through.

Extenders do much the same as insulators, but set the electrified element of the fence out away from your existing fence. Be sure to buy extenders that are safe for horses — while cows are unlikely to run into and hurt themselves on metal extenders, horses may.

Switches

While not necessary for simple layouts or for the small operation, switches that cut power to part of the fence can be helpful when troubleshooting, moving parts of the fence, or if your complex layout requires power to one fenced area but not another. Switches also allow you to turn off the current to the fence from out in the field and save trips back and forth to the energizer. This is useful when you are working on the fence and your charger is indoors, or on long fences. Switches are often attached to end posts and cost from $6 to $9.

Wind-up reels and systems

You can make an inexpensive wind-up reel from materials obtained from the hardware store, or, for $20 to $30, you can buy a reel and a wind-up system. Each reel stores a length of your fence (depending on the fence type), and a wind-up system will allow you to exchange a

full reel for an empty one when taking up your fence. Reels and systems can include a mechanism for locking the reel to prevent unwinding and a neck strap to transfer some of the weight from your arms. Reels get heavy on long stretches of fencing, so we recommend a neck strap. If you are going to be moving your fence often, we recommend the labor-saving, frustration-saving beauty of a well-made reel and winding system.

Electricity

Portable batteries can be used for charging smaller fences.

Electric current flows from your power source (house current, battery or solar collector) to the fence energizer. House current is AC (alternating current), while batteries and solar collectors store current as DC (direct current). The DC stored by the energizer is gathered approximately each second, and ready to flow through the conductor (the fence wire, tape etc.) Available energy is measured in joules.

When you set up the fence, you run a wire from the port labeled "ground" to a rod that goes deep into the soil. When a horse touches the fence with his nose, the readied current travels through him from nose to feet. It then travels through the ground to the ground rod, up to the energizer, and thus completes the circuit. The shock the horse feels is the electricity going through him as the circuit is completed. When shocked by an electric fence, horses will startle and shy away. If you are shocked by the same fence, you might find yourself propelled backward — the electricity causes your muscles to contract, which is why you stiffen and may fall to the ground.

If your fence wire touches high grass, bushes or snow, the current will travel through these to the ground and won't shock the horse. Some fencers are advertised to "shock through wet weeds," which means that you can get by with some high grass and still shock the horse.

Energizers (chargers)

Chargers vary by output size (joules), and they vary by input type: battery, 110 volt AC (house current), and solar. They also vary by output performance curves (high-impedance, low-impedance, or wide-impedance).

While the output in joules is the most accurate way to measure the output of the fence, it is not the only criteria in effectiveness. Some manufacturers advertise their energizers by joules, and others compare them by the number of miles of fencing that can effectively be charged. The latter is under ideal conditions and useful for comparisons, but it can vary widely depending on your set-up.

The energizer best for your operation depends on many factors. The longer the fence you need to energize, and the more wires strung on the fence, the more powerful the unit must be. The climate influences your choice because wet ground is a better conductor of electricity than dry ground. The soil type also influences how well current will travel back to the ground rod. The conductor influences your choice because thicker gauges and some types of wire (and the connecting plastics) can handle more current than others.

If your fence is permanent, you'll choose a different energizer than if your fence is semi-permanent or temporary. If the vegetation alongside and under your fence is likely to be high, you'll choose a different unit than if this vegetation is mowed or grazed. Some energizers are designed for use outside, while others require the shelter of a building or some homemade structure.

High-impedance energizers make more energy available all the time. Reportedly, these don't perform as well in high-grass situations because they short out more easily. Low-impedance energizers are often recommended or required (to avoid voiding the warranty) for some types of fence conductors that will otherwise burn out. These are still effective. The newest type of energizer is wide-impedance, also called "adjustable loading" or with "multiple level electronic gearing." These energizers are more versatile in high grass on dry soil, and with a wider range of conductors. They are also more expensive.

Batteries

The smaller fence energizers require four or six D-cell batteries. These energizers are lightweight and easy to use, but larger batteries are effective for a longer period of time. Twelve-volt car batteries can be used for some energizers; these work well as long as you allow them to discharge to about 80 percent of capacity before recharging (otherwise you ruin the battery). Deep-cycle (marine-type) 12-volt batteries may also be used with some energizers, and these can be discharged to 40 percent before recharging without harm.

Grounding the fence

The ground rod is a metal rod or post (usually galvanized steel) driven into the soil. It completes the circuit from the soil (with the help of moisture in the soil), through the ground wire, to the negative terminal of the energizer.

Ground rods also channel lightning into the ground. They can be placed along the length of the fence to allow lightning to discharge into the soil, reducing the risk of energizer damage.

Failure of the ground device is a common cause of failure in electric fencing. In areas with reasonable moisture and plant material, a single six-foot rod at the fence power point may be sufficient. A three-foot rod may be effective in wet ground.

If your fence charger is placed permanently, you might want to install a more permanent and more reliable ground system. You can use three eight-foot ground rods driven eight feet apart and connect your charger to a wire coming off these.

Or, for stronger applications, dig a 12-foot trench eight inches deep across the direction of the fence line near the charger. Drive three eight-foot, ½" diameter galvanized rods into the trench, one at each end and one in the middle. Use brass ground-rod clamps to connect the three rods together and then to the negative (ground) side of the fence charger with high-voltage wire. Ground-rod packages are sold by some manufacturers.

For safety's sake, place the ground rods outside the pasture or paddock to avoid horse contact. Do not place ground rods within 50 feet of buried metal water, utility or phone lines, or metal stock tanks. Do not use water lines or existing AC ground rods for fence grounding. For best results, always follow the manufacturer's directions.

Gates

We recommend conventional gates for high-traffic areas; these are much safer and easier to handle than electric gates, particularly for children, visitors and clients. Opening an electric-wire gate and leading a wary horse out, while trying to keep the rest of the horses inside, can be extremely challenging.

If you electrify a line (versus a continuous loop) of fence and place your charger on the gate handle side of the line, the gate will be electricity free when open. This is easier for us to handle, but the horses don't know the difference, hence you must

exercise caution to keep the wire gate wide open.

Spring-type gates are available, which compress up against the gate post out of the way, and if made highly visible by flagging, these can work well. The simplest and least expensive plastic gate handles work fine for under $4 investment.

Testers

Simple pocket testers that tell you that your fence is working (or not) cost as little as a few dollars. Complex testers measure the output more accurately and sell for as much as $70. We recommend a mid-priced tester to take the guesswork out of your electrical system.

A simple test of the line will tell you whether current is traveling through it or if it has grounded out between the charger and that part of the fence.

How much will it cost?

Wire
The smaller the gauge, the bigger the wire; bigger wire is more expensive.
　　　Steel or galvanized steel 1¢ - 3¢/ft.

Poly twisted/braided with wire
Stronger will be the more expensive of the prices.
　　　2¢ - 4¢/ft.

Rope　*1/4", poly & copper 15¢/ft.*
　　　　3/8", poly, copper & tin alloy 4¢/ft.

Tape　*1/2" 3¢ - 6¢/ft.; 3/4" 6¢/ft.; 1½" 9¢ - 17¢/ft.*

Board　*$1.50 - $2.35/ft.*

Posts　*fiberglass $2.30 - $3.95 each; step-in $2.30 - $2.65 each; board $9.21 each*

Chargers
Note that these are price ranges. Distances are given for reference if known. Distances are as advertised by manufacturer under optimum conditions and give relative strengths, but may not be accurate under typical operating situations — such as high weeds, etc.

Low impedance
Battery	6-volt	$92 - $130 (25 miles)
	12-volt	$96 - $150 (25 miles)
Solar	6-volt	$160 (5 miles); $240 (25 miles)
	12-volt	$342 (30 miles); $360 (35 miles)
AC		$91 - $110 (30 miles);
		$126 (50 miles);
		$150 - $247 (75 miles);
		$320 (150 miles)

High impedance
Battery	6-volt	(takes 4 D-cells) $85
	9-volt	(takes 6 D-cells) $112
	12-volt	$82 (10 miles)
Solar	6-volt	$203 (25 miles)
AC		$55 (6 miles); $85 (4 - 20 miles);
		$105 (8 miles); $245 (10 miles);
		$300 (20 miles)

Adjustable-loading, or wide-impedance, or 3-level electronic-gearing battery
These self-adjust their power according to the need, reducing energy drain under optimum conditions.

Battery	12-volt	$180 - $349 - $495
AC		$385 (40 miles); $592 (80 miles);
		$700 (110 miles) PH

14

Manure Spreaders

With the average horse producing 50 pounds of manure a day, no horseman needs to be told that disposing of manure can be a challenge.

Manure disposal can be handled a number of ways, including composting, having it hauled away and spreading it yourself. Because composting takes time and space — and can quickly grow into more compost than you could possibly need for the next hundred years — and having manure hauled away is filled with drawbacks, we're going to focus on the most logical solution for many horse owners: spreading the stuff on your own land.

Mini manure spreaders are a handy size — just right for a small barn. The Millcreek Spreader is shown here.

Spreader specs

We believe manure should be spread daily, so for many horse own-ers, this means using a "mini" manure spreader, which is general-ly adequate for a one- to four-horse farm. These spreaders hold around 25 bushels or 28 cubic feet, when the manure is heaped. You should take manufacturer's estimated spreader loads with a grain of salt. One man's version of a "heaped" load may not be the same as someone else's. While you can purchase larger spreaders and let them sit for a few days until they are full before you empty them, we feel this can cause a number of problems, even if the spreader is left under cover, due to the acidity of the urine.

Even under the best of circumstances, manure will eventually de-teriorate whatever we put it in, whether it's wood or metal (plastic, however, is virtually indestructible). Leaving a spreader outside while partially full, especially in freezing weather, is asking for trou-ble. Rain and snow will get into the manure, making it heavier and more difficult to spread.

Don't fill a spreader with densely packed manure or allow ma-nure to freeze in your spreader. Manufacturers report — and we agree — that you're going to break something on your spreader if you try to empty it while the contents are still frozen. Even leaving a spreader outside empty can cause problems in freezing weather. The snow and ice cover the spreader mechanisms and freeze, some-times solidly enough that the mechanisms can't operate properly and may break under the stress. And jamming your spreader full of densely packed manure, such as that found in run-in sheds that are cleaned out annually "whether they need it or not" or in manure piles that have settled for some time, runs you the likely risk of bro-ken chains or other parts.

The Fuerst Spreader can be pulled by a 9 horsepower tractor.

Few, if any mini manure spreaders come with a tail gate. The Country Manufacturer is shown here.

Finally, we feel filling the spreader and letting it sit defeats some of the purpose of having a spreader. It becomes similar to having a manure pile: It's unattractive and a breeding place for flies.

We appreciate spreaders that don't require a large tractor, which can cost as much as an automobile or more. Plus, as they weigh only 250 to 335 pounds, a small spreader can be moved slightly out of the way without hooking it up to the lawn tractor, if necessary. And, although mini-spreaders come without a tongue rest or kick stand (we recommend letting the tongue rest on a concrete block when not in use), hitching them to the lawn tractor usually doesn't require a lot of strength.

With ground-driven mini spreaders, the movement of the wheels provides the power that moves the spreader mechanisms. Larger spreaders often require that the pulling vehicle have a power take-off (PTO). A PTO spreader's power is provided via the spreader's PTO shaft, which is connected to the PTO located on the back of the tractor.

Your ground-driven mini manure spreader will not spread manure until you engage the spreading mechanism. When you do this, the chains along the floor of the spreader move the manure toward the back of the spreader, where the beater grabs the manure and flings it off the back of the spreader, dispersing it on your fields. We like spreaders that allow you to engage and disengage the mechanisms from the seat of the tractor if you can reach it. It's simpler and faster.

Tires are especially important in a ground-driven spreader, since if they don't turn, the spreader doesn't operate. While on dry surfaces most tires will perform adequately, we prefer tires with deep-gripping treads, which should provide better traction in muddy or snowy environments. Of course, if your towing vehicle won't go through the accumulated snow or mud, you will be unable to use your spreader anyway.

Floors are especially important to us when choosing a manure spreader, since they are usually the most major thing to deteriorate on the spreader (chains will also break and wear out with time, but they are relatively easy to replace). We are partial to poly floors because they won't corrode and rot. The choice of material for the remainder of the construction of the spreader may be an arguable point, since it doesn't take as much abuse from moisture and the amount of wear as the floor.

Since purchasing a large tractor for just spreading manure is not in many budgets, we think mini manure spreaders may be a good choice for many small horse farms.

Safety counts

A little common sense goes a long way when operating tractors and manure spreaders around horses.

■ *Avoid walking your horse down a barn aisle that has a manure spreader parked in it, even if it appears that there's "plenty of room."*

■ *Never start a lawn tractor near a horse, unless he's accustomed to the noise, especially if the horse is tied or crosstied.*

■ *Don't clean your stalls with the horse loose in the stall and the manure spreader right outside the door (he may try to bolt over it or squeeze between the door and the spreader). Instead, tie your horse to the back of the stall and work safely around him or move him to another stall while you clean his.*

■ *Never engage your spreader until you are certain it is clear of people, horses and pets. Always turn the spreader off once it is emptied and you are returning to the barn area.*

■ *When spreading manure in a field with horses, keep one eye on the horses to be sure they don't follow the spreader, getting debris in their eyes.*

Think you're giving away a gold mine?

We all know manure is good fertilizer, so it would seem that gardeners and landscapers would come banging on your door to get some "free horse manure." Think again. While some folks are lucky enough to have a nearby greenhouse or nursery who needs a constant supply of manure, for the most part you literally can't give it away. And even if you can, you probably don't want a constant flow of traffic on and off your premises from one-garden owners.

Some companies will haul your manure on a regular basis, but it's pricey. And there may be rules. Refuse companies may insist you load the manure into a dumpster they pro-

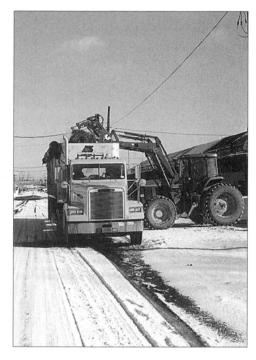

Having manure hauled away can be inconvenient, noisy and expensive.

vide on your facilities that they empty regularly. Other companies may load the manure and haul it away for you, but they may have specific requirements on how you store or stack it and exactly what you bed with. While mushroom growers have become "famous" in the horse industry for wanting horse manure, they only want straw. Mushrooms don't grow well in shavings/sawdust, which is what many of us use as bedding.

And if you have the manure hauled away, you need a place to store it. Manure piles are smelly and unsightly, and you don't want them in the same field with your horses, who invariably will go exploring in the pile for snips of leftover hay. Try to place your manure piles on a hill away from the barn and running water (or your well!). This way, water drains downhill out of the pile, and fly problems in the barn are minimized.

Daily chores

Obviously, stalls, pens and run-in sheds must be cleaned daily, not only for aesthetic reasons but, more importantly, for health reasons. Manure and urine can wreak havoc on a horse's lungs and hooves. The ammonia in urine irritates lung linings, which can cause heaves, and wet, dirty bedding is a breeding ground for bacteria, which can cause thrush.

Cleaning a stall is basically a simple process of taking out the waste and leaving the clean bedding. If you clean the same horse's stall each day, you become familiar with his usual dirty areas and can watch for indications that the horse is not feeling up to par. If an individual horse's stall is abnormally messy, it may indicate that the horse is suffering from diarrhea. If there is evidence of stall walking or pawing, the horse may have been frightened during the night or had a mild bout with colic. (If the stall is relatively free of manure or only has a few hard pieces of manure and your horse looks distressed, the horse may be suffering from an intestinal blockage or colic. If you suspect this, contact your veterinarian immediately.) You should also inspect walls for signs of rubbing, chewing or kicking, and note whether or not the horse has consumed all his hay, feed and a normal amount of water. When all the unwanted waste has been removed from the stall, you're ready to dispose of the manure.

Just as you clean stalls every day, the manure should be spread or disposed of daily.

Where To Spread: *On an ideal horse farm, you will have a separate field for spreading manure, rather than spreading it in the same field with the horses. As you know, manure contains worm eggs, and if your horse eats the grass surrounding the freshly spread manure he's likely to ingest those eggs, reinfecting himself. Fortunately, regular deworming with a good broad-spectrum dewormer, like ivermectin, minimizes this problem.*

You can spread manure by hand, but it's a tiresome, messy job.

In real life, most of us don't own enough land to spread the manure away from the horses. When spreading manure on your pasture, take care to only spread it on established grasses. Fresh manure is highly acidic and can destroy bushes, plants, young trees and young grass. Of course, properly dried or composted, it does make a good, natural fertilizer. Always spread the manure as thinly as possible to expedite drying. As the manure dries, the worm eggs die and the manure smell will dissipate more quickly. Thinly spread manure is also less noticeable visually to neighbors.

Try to spread the manure in the farthest corner of the field or the least-favorite grazing area of your horses. Rotate where you spread, so the layers stay thin. Manure that is spread thinly will break down and rot into the soil more quickly. We would also advise spreading the manure, if possible, when your horses are not turned out, as invariably they may wander over to see what you're doing.

Never spread manure in your riding arena. While it may seem that sawdust bedding would make wonderful footing,

Piling manure in the horse's field is unhealthy, as horses may be tempted to pick through the pile looking for left-over hay.

in reality it can be slippery when wet, especially if it has a high content of manure. And it's not healthy due to the dust that is generated in normal arena use.

Manure also isn't a good option for traction over icy sur-faces. Not only will it eventually work down into the dirt, creating a nearly permanent boggy footing, it will insu-late the ice from the warming sun, so the icy surface lasts longer. (Kitty litter or sand are much better options for traction.) ■PH■

15

Getting Hitched

To reduce the hazards of horse-hauling, our trailer-hitch hints and guidelines can help you make a safe connection between your trailer and tow vehicle.

Our forefathers would probably be shocked at the change in meaning of "travel with horses." Back then traveling with horses meant the horse hauled us. Today, we're usually the ones hauling the horses, to trail rides and horse shows. But, before you fire up the "horsepower" under your hood and hurry down the highway with horses in tow, you must first have a trustworthy trailer hitch.

Before you buy a hitch

The world's biggest, heaviest-duty hitch won't affect the single most important factor in towing — your vehicle's maximum towing capacity (that is, how much weight your vehicle can pull). Officially called its Gross Combination Weight Rating, your vehicle's maximum tow capacity is the first thing you must know before you select a hitch. Of course, the larger your trailer and the more horses you haul, the more tow capacity your vehicle needs. Never try to pull more weight than your vehicle's GCWR as listed in your vehicle's owner's manual (or call your nearest dealership).

Clearly, you also need to know how much weight you routinely haul. An average-sized all-steel two-horse trailer weighs from about 3,000 to 3,700 pounds. A 16-foot all-steel stock trailer generally weighs between 3,500 and 4,000 pounds. All-aluminum trailers

Installing a trailer hitch can be a do-it-yourself project, or you can let professionals tackle the job.

usually weigh several hundred pounds less (up to one-third less) than their all-steel counterparts. Still, with two or three 1,000-pound horses, plus tack and a few bales of hay, your total tow weight will easily exceed 5,000 pounds.

For an accurate estimate of your typical tow weight, take your loaded trailer to a commercial weigh station. For the truest reading, raise the trailer up off the ball, since some of the trailer's weight rests on the hitch.

Which hitch?

Three basic categories of horse-trailer hitches allow you to tailor your set-up to match your towing needs. The basic weight-carrying hitch, attached to the tow vehicle's rear underside frame, is the most common hitch for pulling light-to-medium-weight tag-along trailers (up to about 5,000 pounds gross weight). The weight-distributing hitch is designed for heavier tag-along trailers. The gooseneck hitch is used only in open-bed pickup trucks.

Some vehicles have a pre-drilled hole in the rear bumper for a tow ball and are weight-rated to carry up to 5,000 pounds (hence, the nickname "bumper-pull trailers"). For safety reasons, however, hitching your horse trailer directly to a ball on your bumper is never recommended.

What's the hitch?

For tag-along trailers, the largest hitch component is the receiver, which bolts to your vehicle's underside frame. Hitch receivers (which "receive" the hitch ball mount) are classed by weight capacity. Most American-made horse trailers require, at minimum, a Class III receiver, which can pull 5,000-6,000 pounds loaded trailer weight (depending on the hitch brand). The same receiver paired with a weight-distributing hitch (promoting it to a Class IV receiver) can pull 10,000-12,000 pounds.

Some manufacturers produce a heavier-duty receiver, rated to carry 7,500 to 8,000 pounds without weight-distributing. However, these hitches are designed primarily for full-size trucks, which can handle the extra tongue weight, and they often require a more expensive, heavy-duty ball mount as well. They are not designed for for sports utility vehicles (SUVs).

The second key element in your hitch package is the ball mount, which slides into the receiver and locks in place with a locking pin. Ball mounts vary in length — rise/drop measurements — to bridge any difference in height between the hitch receiver and the tongue of the trailer (four-wheel drive vehicles tend to "sit up" higher, for instance, and usually require a deeper "drop" in the ball mount). Some hitch makers offer adjustable ball mounts, convenient for towing trailers of various coupler heights with the same vehicle.

Selecting the appropriate ball mount is crucial to keeping your trailer level. At a standstill, both your towing vehicle and loaded trailer should be horizontal, with no slope. If your trailer tilts, either forward or backward, you need a different length ball mount to level it. However, if your tow vehicle sags in the rear, the tongue weight is too heavy, and you'll likely need a weight-distributing hitch (explained below).

The primary connection between your vehicle and your trailer is the hitch ball. Typically made of solid steel, balls are often available in a variety of finishes, such as chrome or zinc, which help prevent rust. Hitch balls are always weight-rated, based on diameter, shank length and shank diameter. The most common ball diameter for tag-along trailers is 2". A bigger ball will carry more weight. The ball's load rating is stamped on the top of the ball —

make sure the ball you choose meets or exceeds your anticipated gross trailer weight.

The ball must fit snugly into the trailer's coupler; if the ball is too small, the coupler could bounce off at the first big bump in the road. If the ball is too large, either the coupler won't settle down onto it, or you won't be able to lock it down. Wear and tear can also affect tightness of fit.

When attaching the hitch ball to the ball mount, be sure not to overtighten or undertighten the hitch-ball nut on the shank. If too loose, the nut can work its way off. But overtightening can cause thread damage, with potential ball-shank failure. Manufacturers typically recommend a specific tightness (or "torque"), so always use a torque wrench, not an impact wrench, to tighten your ball down.

Some manufacturers offer a convertible ball-head design (such as Valley's Adapt-A-Ball), which allows you to change ball sizes (when you need to pull a trailer with a different size coupler) without removing the shaft and torquing down a new ball. All you need is a screwdriver to change ball heads.

Gooseneck hitches, which mount in the back of an open-bed truck, are available in a variety of styles. The standard stationary hitch is a 25/16" ball on a metal plate that bolts down through the truck bed into the underside frame. Some styles allow you to either remove the ball when not in use or fold it down into a small box flush with the bed, a convenient feature if you need to haul wood or feed bags in the back of your truck.

Get to know your towing terms

Gross Combination Weight Rating (GCWR) is the maximum allowable weight, expressed in pounds, that your towing vehicle can safely pull without costly damage to the vehicle's powertrain. The GCWR includes the fully loaded vehicle (fuel, driver and all passengers, gear/supplies) plus the fully loaded trailer, hitch weight and all other additional equipment.

Loaded tow weight is the total weight of your fully loaded trailer, including horses, feed, water and tack. The trailer's "dry," or empty, weight is usually stamped on the vehicle identification tag (usually attached to the left front of the trailer frame); it's also listed on the Manufacturer's Statement of Origin, with its registration.

Tongue weight *is the amount of the trailer's weight which is transferred down onto the tow ball of the towing vehicle (typically, 10 to 15 percent of the gross trailer weight with tag-along trailers; 25 percent with goosenecks). With tag-along trailers, too much weight can slightly lift the tow vehicle's front axle,*

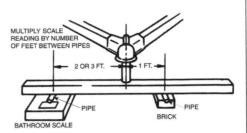

reducing steering response and braking control; too little weight can lift the rear of the vehicle, reducing rear-wheel traction and contributing to trailer sway, especially on highways, rough roads and curves. You can measure your trailer's tongue weight at a commercial weigh station or on a bathroom scale, as illustrated above.

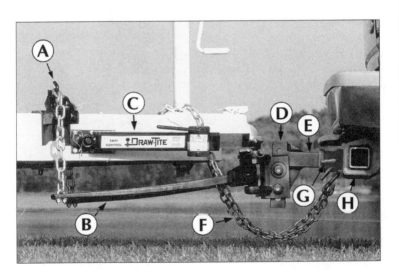

A weight-distributing system includes:

A Lift-Lock II™ hook-
* up bracket kits*
B Spring bars
C Sway control (optional)
D Head

E Shank
F Safety chains
G Pin and clip
H Receiver hitch

Hitch helpers

If your vehicle's rear end squats under the weight of your tag-along trailer, you need a weight-distributing hitch. A sagging rear end on your tow vehicle creates a light front end, making it tougher to both steer and stop. A weight-distributing (or "equalizing") hitch spreads the trailer's tongue weight over the frames and axles of both vehicle and trailer. The more evenly the weight is distributed, the more solidly your vehicle and trailer tires will hold the ground for optimum traction and control.

In general, weight-distributing hitches are recommended for any gross trailer weight over 5,000 pounds. You may especially need a weight-distributing hitch if your tow vehicle has a relatively short wheelbase (114" is the recommended bare minimum for towing; 131" and above is better) or if you're towing close to your vehicle's maximum weight. Typically, a weight-distributing hitch doubles the tow weight and tongue weight your receiver hitch can safely handle.

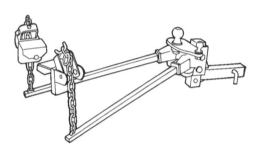

A weight distributing hitch, such as the trunnion-bar style shown above, can significantly improve traction, steering and braking control.

(It does not, however, increase your tow vehicle's maximum tow rating — again, regardless of your hitch capacity, never try to pull more than your vehicle can safely handle.)

A weight-distributing hitch slides into your tow vehicle's receiver, replacing the ball mount. The system consists of two "equalizing" bars that attach to the trailer tongue with chains and snap-up brackets (see drawing above). As you tighten the spring bars, the hitch point lifts, leveling the tongue weight over all wheels of the tow vehicle and trailer.

Weight-distributing hitches are available in two styles: round-bar and trunnion. Although trunnion bars can usually hold slightly more weight, the difference between the two is largely aesthetic (whether you prefer the look of round bars or square ones).

For all their benefits, weight-distributing hitches do pose a couple of drawbacks. First, at about $300 and up, they're a fairly costly addition to your basic receiver. Also, they're often troublesome to install and must be removed from the trailer and hitch receiver after each use.

In addition to weight distribution, your particular truck/trailer configuration may also need a sway-control device (about $100). Sway controls help dampen the fishtailing effects of crosswinds, rough roads and nervous nellies dancing around in back of the trailer. Specially designed to reduce a trailer's side-to-side motion, most sway controls use a sliding-friction device, much like a brake pad, to cut down sideward movement.

Hitch makers recommend using a single sway control on trailers under about 26-feet long (installed on the passenger's side of the trailer tongue); on longer trailers, consider using two sway controls, one on each side.

Use safety chains safely

It's a horse owner's worst nightmare. You're driving down the road when you hit a deep pothole. The coupler bounces off the ball, the safety chains' S-hooks jerk out of their holes and, suddenly, your loose trailer — with your horses trapped inside — is careening off the road-side or into the path of oncoming traffic. Granted, it doesn't hap-

Whenever possible, replace S-hooks on safety chains (as shown here), with French links, which can provide a safer connection.

pen often, but when it does, it can be disastrous.

Hitch makers agree: S-hooks are, at best, the lazy way to attach a safety chain, and at worst, downright dangerous. If your trailer's safety chains are equipped with S-hooks, replace them with quick links (also called French links), which provide a "positive closure." To properly attach your safety chains, pass them through the chain bracket holes on the hitch receiver and use the quick links to securely attach the chains back to themselves.

Hitching up your hitch

For the mechanically inclined, hitch installation can be a cost-effective do-it-yourself project. Receivers, ball mounts and balls are sold at most farm stores, auto supply shops, hardware stores and RV/camping stores.

Your first choice will be between a multi-fit receiver (designed to fit a number of different vehicles) or a custom-fit receiver (specifically made for a certain vehicle frame style). Multi-fit receivers are often less expensive, but they usually require some assembly (the arm brackets must be adjusted, width-wise, to fit each vehicle's framing). They may also require drilling holes in the vehicle frame, so they're often more difficult and time-consuming to install. Also, much like one-size-fits-all clothing, multi-fit hitches look better on some vehicles than on others.

Custom-fit hitches, on the other hand, are designed for specific vehicles. Usually a single welded piece, with no side-arm adjustments, a custom hitch is also easier to install, generally needing no drilling into the vehicle frame.

Many stores keep multi-fit Class III hitches in-stock, as well as a few of their most popular-selling custom-fit hitches. Most stores will also special-order less common custom-fit hitches, although special orders are seldom available same-day. Multi-fit hitches typically cost around $100; custom-fit hitches range widely, from $75 to $270.

Make sure both your vehicle and your trailer remain level — horizontal to the ground, with no tilting or sagging — when your trailer is fully loaded. If they're not, you may need a weight distributing hitch.

Ball mounts and balls are sold separately. Depending on weight rating and rise/drop measurements, ball mounts cost from $16 to $50. Hitch balls usually cost about $8 to $20.

Keep in mind, hitch installation can be strenuous work. Class III receivers are quite heavy (on average, about 50 to 60 pounds) and unwieldy to hold and bolt while you're lying flat on your back under your vehicle. Most do-it-yourselfers need an assistant and about one to two hours time, depending on whether you bought a no-drill model or not. Professional hitch installers suggest using a hydraulic jack to hold the receiver firmly in place.

If you're proficient with a drill and/or metal saw, installing a gooseneck hitch can also be a do-it-yourself project. With any hitch style, you'll need to drill through the bed of your truck and down into the frame; if you choose a hide-away style, you'll have to cut a hole in your truck bed, plus do some drilling.

THE WORLD'S BIGGEST, HEAVIEST-DUTY HITCH WON'T AFFECT THE SINGLE MOST IMPORTANT FACTOR IN TOWING — YOUR VEHICLE'S MAXIMUM TOWING CAPACITY (THAT IS, HOW MUCH WEIGHT YOUR VEHICLE CAN PULL).

Rather not do it yourself? Try your nearest trailer dealer or auto mechanic. Of course, you'll pay more (our informal market survey indicated that, on top of the cost of the hitch, installation fees usually start from $40), but if you don't already have a decent drill, a half-inch drill bit and a torque wrench, then letting a professional do it could save you money.

You can also take your vehicle to your local branch of U-Haul, the world's largest installer of permanent trailer hitches. Not only are U-Haul's prices reasonable (receivers from about $100; labor fees from $17.50), an additional $5 ensures a lifetime "All-Hazard" warranty on every hitch installed at any of its 1,100 U-Haul Centers across the United States and Canada (the company also has nearly 14,000 independent dealers, who may or may not offer the warranty, so be sure to ask first). If the hitch is damaged for any reason — like collision, corrosion, accidental overload, jack-knife or vehicle theft — U-Haul will replace it free of charge for as long as you own the vehicle.

If you're buying a new tow vehicle, most trucks, vans and SUVs can be ordered with a special towing package, which typically includes a larger engine and radiator, heavier frame, stiffer suspension, heavy-duty shocks and springs, larger mirrors, and possibly a hitch receiver. If the receiver is not part of the factory-installed package, the dealership's service department will often install a hitch for you.

Protecting your hitch ball

Not only an eyesore on your tow vehicle, a rusty hitch ball can also cause wear and tear inside your trailer coupler, with grating friction at every turn. Yes, you can slap a little lubricant on the ball before you hitch up the trailer and, later, slip an old tennis ball over the naked ball. But, instead, experts recommend doing what the receiver hitch was specifically designed to allow: Take the ball mount off the receiver when you're not using it. In addition to preventing corrosion of the mount and ball, mount removal also eliminates shin-banging — and hitch grease on your pants.

Hitch makers

While industry research indicates that only about 20 percent of people who tow trailers have the slightest name-brand awareness of hitches, brand names do carry weight with car manufacturers, hitch installers and trailer dealers. Although every hitch on the market has passed certain standards set by the Society of Automotive Engineers, manufacturers are allowed to conduct their own product testing, without independent verification. Consequently, since product failure could pose an enormous liability in an accident, hitch makers are careful to produce sturdy, dependable products.

Professional hitch installers, however, often have distinct brand preferences, based on their own experiences with product quality, reliability and ease of installation. By far, the "Big Three" on the market are Valley, Draw-Tite and Reese, with several smaller national and regional competitors including Shelton, Quality S, Hidden Hitch and others.

■ Valley Industries

One of the nation's largest hitch manufacturers, Valley supplies original-equipment hitches for most major car makers in the country, including General Motors, Ford and Dodge. Consequently, Valley is often the first maker on the market with custom hitches for late-model vehicles. That's one reason why many hitch installers and retailers (including U-Haul, Ace Hardware, Redneck Trailers, NAPA Automotive Stores, Pep Boys Automotive, AutoZone and Tractor Supply Company) also carry the Valley brand.

■ Draw-Tite, Inc.

With 52 years' experience, Draw-Tite supplies hitches to over 10,000 independent hitch retailers and installers, making it the country's largest "after-market" hitch maker. And, although Draw-Tite cheerfully admits that their products are 20 to 40 percent more expensive than their competitors, our market survey showed that Draw-Tite is a top favorite with professional hitch installers. The company is also a major supplier to U-Haul.

Draw-Tite's extensive testing procedures simulate real-life situations, like panic stops, sharp turns, accelerations into traffic, and jarring bumps over potholes and railroad tracks. However, for a Draw-Tite hitch, you'll probably need to take your vehicle to U-Haul or another installer, since the company doesn't sell to big retailers (like automotive or farm-store chains).

■ Reese

The company that originally designed and developed today's receiver hitch (which replaced the old "shin-banger" hitch with a nonremovable ball mount), Reese enjoys top name-brand awareness among many hitch installers and dealers. A sister company of Draw-Tite's, Reese makes original custom equipment for some car manufacturers, as well as hitches for mass merchandisers.

■ Shelton Industries

Though one of the industry's smaller manufacturers, Shelton Industries is a major hitch supplier for several large farm supply stores. The company recently introduced a new Lock-A-Link hitch system, which replaces the standard ball mount and safety chains on a tag-along trailer. The patented double-lock design features a castle-nut lock system to hold the mount into the receiver, plus a safety chain that locks onto the mount (the links can't bounce off or straighten out). Though pricey ($139 list price), the Lock-A-Link system offers added peace of mind for horse-haulers.

Our recommendations

According to hitch manufacturers and trailer dealers, few hitch failures are caused by poor product quality. Instead, accidents are most often caused by user errors — such as overtightening or undertightening the hitch ball and failing to properly lock the hitch pin or trailer coupler.

Regardless of brand, your primary concern when selecting hitch components is weight capacity. Experts recommend installing a hitch that's over-rated for your needs (don't buy the bare minimum you can get by with). Also keep in mind, your hitch is only as strong as its weakest component; for instance, you can only pull 5,000 pounds with a ball rated for 5,000 pounds, even if it's mounted on a Class IV heavy-duty receiver with a weight-carrying capacity of 8,000 pounds.

Remember, you've got a lot riding on your trailer hitch. As one hitch maker commented to us, "Hauling horses is a huge responsibility. We're talking safety here — not only for you and your horses, but for everyone else on the road around you." So always, on each and every trip, triple-check your hitch connections. Much as we once relied on our trusty steeds to transport our families safely to our destination, your horses' safety now rests with you. PH

16

Finding A
Cross-Country Shipper

*When you have to ship your horse
across the country commercially,
it's important to know what questions to ask.*

You just landed the job you've always wanted in another state, and there's a great place for your horses right down the road. The only challenge now is to move them to their new home. The questions you ask when investigating shippers may mean the difference between a comfortable situation for you and your horses and an experience you won't want to repeat. For some questions, the dispatcher can provide information, but for others, a driver is your best source for accurate information.

We asked questions of a cross-section of shippers and horse-owners in researching this chapter, and we suggest you do the same. Don't limit your calling around to national carriers. Some mom-and-pop operations give wonderful personalized care.

Questions to ask

What is your most frequently traveled route?
You may save time and money by choosing a carrier that routinely operates between you and your horse's destination. Other carriers will go your direction as soon as they can contract for enough horses to fill their load, and still others do such a volume of business that they will take your horses from door to door with as little as a few hours notice, even if there are no others traveling your way.

Some shipping companies not only ship door-to-door, but also pick up at the airport and deliver to your farm or quarantine station.

Do you contract with other carriers?

If the answer is yes, this means that the initial transportation company may arrange for part of your horse's travel (usually the beginning or end) by a second company. If you're off the beaten path, or going diagonally from Oregon to Alabama, using more than one carrier may be your only choice.

Some companies stay close to the interstate highways and rely on other carriers to provide door-to-door service off their route. Others contract in order to be able to offer their customers more routes and more distant destinations. This arrangement may or may not increase your rate — some initial carriers get a percentage of the subcontractor's fee — so you'll want to call more than one company and compare rates.

If you prefer to make your own arrangements, most carriers who can't take you door to door will refer you to other carriers with whom they've had good experience. For example, members of the National Horse Carriers Association will recommend other NHCA members. We also found carriers who prefer not to hand your horse off to others because they choose to be solely responsible for your horse's well being.

Do you guarantee the route?

A guaranteed route means that once the travel plan is made, the carrier won't deviate to pick up any additional horses. This is an advantage — you know exactly where your horse will travel and can plan on the arrival without his having spent an extra night deviating from the presumed route. However, if you are the owner who needs a horse picked up and shipped at the last minute, the carrier that does deviate might meet your needs faster. Of the carriers who deviate, many of them told us that they'll only deviate to a limit, perhaps a couple hours off course, to avoid undue stress to their other passengers.

Can I contact the driver directly during the trip?

In this cellular-phone era, most carriers can call out and be reached along their journey. Many have pagers, too. We prefer to be able to talk with the driver periodically to see how our horses are hauling, particularly since we don't haul often enough to know the drivers personally. In general, the smaller companies with owner/drivers will encourage you to call them during the trip. Other companies will call you a couple of hours before they arrive to pick up or leave a horse, or in an emergency. Some supervisors and drivers prefer to separate driving and talking for safety reasons — so you'll always talk to their dispatcher. If there are two drivers aboard, one might do the telephone work when he's not catching up on sleep for the next leg of the trip. Or, you may decide that, as long as you're notified an hour or so before arrival, no news is good news.

May I call for the current location of my horse? How often do drivers check in?

Several of the companies we contacted have satellite tracking systems aboard the rigs that are connected to the dispatch offices. This gives an accurate location anytime. In other cases, most drivers check in two or three times a day.

Tell me about the experience of your drivers, and how many work on each trip.

When we asked, "Are your drivers experienced?" we were always told "Yes," though we didn't know if that meant experienced drivers or also experienced horse handlers.

However, we found the "tell me about" question elicited more information. The industry has mostly gotten away from drivers who also happen to know about horses. However, handling an 18-wheeler in heavy traffic, or a six-horse trailer on mountain roads,

Some companies accept horses wearing "crash helmets," blankets and/or shipping boots, while others feel there is increased possibility of injury should these not fit properly or slip down.

also requires special expertise. When you call about a certain route and time, you can ask about the specific driver who'll haul your horses. If you're working with an owner/driver or a horseman-who-also-drives, you're likely to get the kind of care he would give his own horses.

What is your typical schedule of stops? What is done for the horses at these stops?

Stops for coffee and to check in with the dispatcher may or may not be taken as opportunities to check the horses. These two questions elicited varied answers that said a great deal about the carriers we surveyed.

Some carriers untie the horses at each stop so they can lower their heads, stretch and clear their upper respiratory systems of dust from the trip. Other carriers prefer not to tie the horses at any time, so the horses are always free to drop their heads.

Some of the carriers use pickup and destination stops to get the other horses out for a break. A few will stop periodically at appropriate places for the purpose of unloading, but this practice is risky unless you have horsemen as drivers and horses who are well-trained in loading.

How can you accommodate my weanling, mare and foal, or stallion's special needs? Do stall partitions reach to the floor? Can I reserve a box stall?

Most carriers have the flexibility to make wider stalls for youngsters who don't tie, and they report that box stalls are increasingly popular even for single adult horses.

While most vans have plenty of head room, some carriers have had custom extra-height trailers made for warmbloods, Saddlebreds and draft horses. Stall partitions are a matter of preference among carriers — some use those that reach to the floor, others prefer the lower span be heavy rubber, and still others use partial partitions for more leg room.

Do you handle other livestock?

This is a good question if you want to send your horse's companion donkey along, and several carriers even accept family dogs and cats.

As one customer cautioned, however, this question is also important if all you're sending is horses. She'd neglected to ask, and her horse was terrified by the addition of several llamas to the van.

Is audio and/or visual contact maintained with the horses?
Given today's technology, we weren't surprised to find nearly half the companies use closed-circuit TV or similar means to monitor horses. We believe the advantages of this outweigh the costs. Particularly on big rigs, one horse struggling may not be felt by even the most experienced of drivers.

Do you accept horses with shipping boots or wrapped bandages?
If you choose to use them, shipping boots can be replaced by the driver with much less risk of tendon injury than wraps. Most carriers we surveyed will not replace wrapped bandages (but will check, and remove them), and many recommend against them because of the chances of them getting wet, slipping or becoming too tight.

Is the rig climate-controlled? How do you handle sheets or blankets?
Depending on your trip and time of year, this may or may not be an issue. The important thing to ascertain from the answer is how aware

the driver is of the temperature inside the rig, and what steps are made to make it more comfortable for the horses. Several carriers give their charges electrolytes during summer trips.

How, and how often, are the horses watered? How do you handle horses who hesitate to drink?

Quite a few of the transporters provide water during the entire trip. Some carry their own water, minimizing taste differences; of those, some use distilled water. Two carriers specifically commented on the horse mentality of "If we're stopped, then I must be getting off" and handled watering either free choice or at the end of longer stops.

May I send my own hay, or, what do you feed?

In nearly every case, we were told that hay is available to horses at all times during the trip. Most of the carriers we polled commented, unprompted, about the importance of minimizing horses' dietary changes. Some carriers minimize their risk by feeding the owners' hay, while others carry a grass/legume mixture typical for the area.

Do you unload during the trip? What precautions are taken at overnight facilities? Do you provide a 24-hour telephone number?

One horse owner told us the horror story of no one at the overnight facility being able to confirm that her horse was there, and a carrier told us his version, which was the inability to reach an owner at night when her horse needed veterinary care. Be sure to exchange 24-hour contact information when you've chosen your carrier.

Some carriers keep only daytime office hours, so don't presume you can just call their office in the evening. When you give them your contact numbers, don't forget your mobile phone or barn phone.

We like the common procedure of leaving horses in the trailer in their own box stall at night because it minimizes contact with diseases and the chance of injury in an unknown facility. Some will open an available adjoining stall in the rig to give your horse more room. Their drivers, like some others, will sleep in the trailer, which assures night-time care if your horse needs it.

Some carriers drive straight through — crossing the country in 2½ to 3½ days — and don't overnight at all, which minimizes disease and unloading/loading problems. Others stop at known stables (often, those of customers) and let the horses out into paddocks. Some utilize recommended horse motels. Still other haulers utilize their own base or hubs as overnight stops. If convenient, you can take your horse to them or pick him up at their base location.

Give the vanning company clear directions to pickup and drop-off locations, realizing that big rigs need adequate driveway space and that you need a safe place to load.

How closely can you predict the time of arrival and drop off? What is your policy for contacting the owner in case of schedule changes?
Some companies use high-tech methods of predicting time of arrival; others a driver's estimate. Most all carriers will have the driver or dispatcher contact you an hour or so ahead of drop-off time. This is in their best interests, scheduling-wise, for each owner to be available to receive her horse.

In the event of an emergency with a horse, what procedures will the driver(s) follow?
Most haulers told us the driver gets medical attention for the horse. Second, he contacts the dispatcher who contacts the owner. The dispatcher gives the owner the veterinarian's phone number, and the customer speaks directly with the vet.

What is your motor carrier (Interstate Commerce Commission, ICC) number? What is your Department of Transportation (DOT) number?
These are regulating agencies; the ICC has more regulations than the DOT. If you choose to ship with registered carriers, you can count on getting those who are knowledgeable of current regulations and restrictions on transport.

Ask the carrier you are considering if they are a member of the National Horse Carriers Association (NHCA). The NHCA (800-967-8267/606-255-9406) is dedicated to maintaining and improving the image of commercial transport companies by disseminating information on transport and transport regulations and to support the carriers through organized and shared operating practices.

Figuring the cost

What will you charge for the trip? What payment arrangements do you require? Does this include my tack trunk? Are there additional charges for difficult driveways? Is there a flat rate to the city and additional charge to the farm? Would it be cheaper if I met you in the nearest town? Do you take credit cards? Do you require a deposit?

We started our research by asking each company to quote a rate for the same hypothetical trip, then we realized the number of factors that go into pricing. The transporter must consider the number of horses over which the fees are divided as well as the number of miles he'll have to travel empty. Some companies charge extra for equipment, others don't. Each shipping situation is so different that you'll do best to ask carriers to quote your exact trip, taking into account number of horses, your preferences on stalls, and the dates.

Our questions revealed base rates from 25 to 50 cents per mile for a single horse in a standing stall; we were quoted approximately 70 cents a mile for mare and foal, draft horse or a horse who needs a double stall. Other carriers were hesitant to give us quotes because they depend on the travel timetable (if you're flexible enough to wait until the carrier has a full load, you can get a lower rate).

Credit cards are ideal for the horse owner who wants to spread the cost of the travel over several months, though some companies will not unload the horse without cash payment. Be careful about putting down a deposit without knowing the reputation of the company; if an unscrupulous company fails to pick up your horse, it can be difficult to get your deposit back.

What services does your shipping contract include?

The shipping contract will be referred to by some companies as the Bill of Lading. Some cover only the minimum of service (transport from origin to destination), and you're given a verbal assurance of more (feeding and watering, checking shipping wraps, etc.). Other contracts are more complete; for example, they give the carrier permission to have your horse treated by a veterinarian.

If written mention is not given of coverage that you desire (feeding schedules, etc.), talk with the company. They may allow you to add items to the contract — or if you check their reputation through references, you may find that they consistently exceed customer service expectations even though it's not in writing. Some shippers will go to great lengths to make sure your horse is ready to haul comfortably.

Horse insurance may or may not be promised (in writing or verbally) by the carrier. Any time you buy insurance, you are entitled to a written binder listing you as the payee. If you already have insurance on your horse, it probably covers mortality or loss of use but not transport or the veterinary work for shipping-related colic. Most carriers are not in the insurance business; we recommend contacting your horse insurance company for a rider that includes the trip if you want insurance.

After arranging for transport insurance, be certain that you add the insurance information to the shipping contract. Most insurance companies require prior approval for procedures like surgery or euthanasia, and it is to your benefit, should you have to collect, if the shipper had this information and has followed the proper procedure.

What paperwork is required?

Check with the company regarding the need for proof of ownership and any other paperwork. At minimum, you'll need a current Coggins and usually a health certificate, so allow two weeks from the time your veterinarian draws the blood sample to receive the papers.

Please provide the names and phone numbers of owners who have hauled with you recently.

While some of the carriers have an impressive list of high-visibility owners as references, those well-known folks may have different needs and standards than you do. Don't be shrugged off by a list of celebrities. Ask for recent customers who live near you, and you're likely to get candid assessments of the carrier's work. Talk with those people about their experience. Sometimes little things that come out in discussion really set your mind at rest.

Our recommendation

Overall, checking references is the single most important thing you can do. If the company won't supple recent references — call the next company. We've heard reports of super service and delivery but we've also heard horror stories. The ultimate responsibility for your horse's care rests with you. ▣PH

Section II

Expert Advice
About
Tack

17

Western Saddle Lingo

Looking to buy a new Western saddle?
Whether you're shopping at your local tack store,
through catalogs or on the Internet, learn the lingo
to select the best saddle for both you and your horse.

To buy a Western saddle these days, you almost need to know a new language. Do you need a rawhide or Ralide tree, with Quarter Horse or semi-Quarter Horse bars? 15", 16" or 17" seat? A double-dee, in-skirt or flat-plate rigging, in full, ⅞ or ¾ position? Oxbow or bell stirrups?

Your choices will be based on several factors, including your horse's conformation (height and slope of his withers and shoulders, the roundness of his ribcage, the length of his back), your own body-build and the activities you plan to pursue in that saddle. And whether you're a serious competitor or just a weekend around-the-farm rider, the right saddle can make a huge difference in comfort and performance for both you and your horse.

To select a saddle style, shape and size that's best suited to meet your needs, you first need to know not only what each part is and its function, but also how it affects your comfort and confidence in the saddle and how it affects the way your horse moves and performs.

Tree terminology

The tree is the underlying framework of any saddle. Its primary parts are the two bars, which rest along either side of the horse's back; the fork, or the front "bridge," which holds the front of the bars together and keeps you from sliding up the horse's neck when he stops

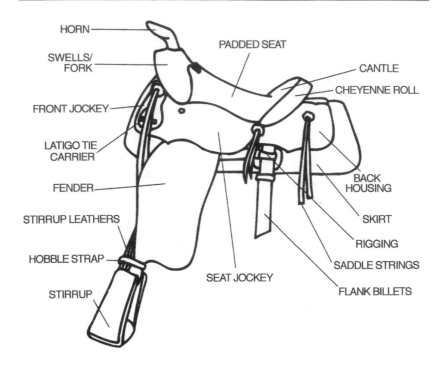

HORN

SWELLS/
FORK

FRONT JOCKEY

LATIGO TIE
CARRIER

FENDER

STIRRUP LEATHERS

HOBBLE STRAP

STIRRUP

PADDED SEAT

CANTLE

CHEYENNE ROLL

BACK
HOUSING

SKIRT

RIGGING

SADDLE STRINGS

FLANK BILLETS

SEAT JOCKEY

suddenly; and the cantle, the back of the saddle seat, which holds both your hindquarters and the back of the bars in proper position.

The shape and width of the fork's swells (on either side of the horn) are largely determined by the saddle's style. Moderate swells on pleasure saddles are about 12 to 13 inches wide, from outer edge to outer edge. Wider, 15-inch swells offer optimum security in the saddle — for instance, when starting a young horse — while roping saddles often have narrower, 9-inch "slick" or "A-fork" swells.

Saddle horns also vary by discipline, from tall, narrow cutting horns to thicker, reinforced roping horns. On pleasure saddles, the horn is more a matter of personal style and preference, since it serves little function.

Cantle shape, height, slope and curvature (or "dish") vary by both sport and rider body-build. In some disciplines, such as barrel racing, a rider may need the extra support of a high cantle; others, such as roping, necessitate a low cantle for quick dismounts. Regardless of height, it's important that the cantle's dish follows the shape of your own hips and legs, and that the cantle ends don't gouge into the back of your thighs. That's something you can judge only by sitting in the saddle and checking for fit.

You'll also often see the term "Cheyenne roll" in conjunction with the cantle. That's the piece of leather that extends, on some saddles, on top of and behind the cantle. Its only purpose is to make the saddle easier to pick up, so whether you want a Cheyenne roll on your new saddle or not is largely based on whether you like its looks or not.

On any saddle, the height of the gullet (the U-shaped channel under the horn and between the swells) should always clear the top of horse's withers by two to three fingers' breadth. It should neither crowd the withers by sitting too low (which means it's too wide) nor sit on top of the withers (too narrow), which could shift your weight too far to the back of the saddle.

Today's trees can be made of wood, fiberglass or molded plastic. A classic wood tree is generally covered with laced or stapled rawhide to strengthen it, but the process of applying the wet rawhide will often shrink and slightly alter the shape of the tree, which means wood trees are not as uniform as synthetic trees. Many high-performance riders, like ropers, look for bullhide-wrapped trees, which are exceptionally strong. Sometimes, wood trees are covered with fiberglass, then coated with a poly resin — the thinner-than-rawhide fiberglass allows closer contact with the horse's back.

One-piece molded-plastic trees — largely dominated by one manufacturer, Ralide — are consistently uniform and very strong; however, they don't have a wood tree's flexibility and "give" when the horse moves. Most economy saddles will have Ralide trees, which are the least expensive type of tree, since they're mass-produced.

To check out the type of tree on any saddle you're considering, lift up a stirrup and peek into the saddle's innards. Look for the seams of a leather-covered wood tree, the "grainy" surface of Ralide or the shiny, varnish-like surface of fiberglass and resin.

Western saddles are generally sold in four tree widths, which are determined by the shape and slope of the tree's bars, as well as by the gullet width (measured from bottom inside edge to bottom inside edge):

■ **Full Quarter Horse**, with a 6½"-wide gullet, designed for stocky, well-muscled horses with low withers.

■ **Thoroughbred** or standard, with a gullet of about 5½", for horses with high, narrow withers.

■ **Semi-Quarter Horse**, with a 6" gullet, for horses built somewhere in between full Quarter Horse and Thoroughbred.

■ **Arabian**, with a gullet of about 6¾", for horses with low, wide withers and short backs.

Each horse has a uniquely shaped back, however, and not all horses conform to their breed's stereotypes, so you can't rely solely on in-store size guidelines — to ensure a good fit, you need to actually try the saddle on your horse.

Sitting-pretty seats

Sized in inches, Western saddle seats are measured from the back of the fork, at the base of the horn, across to the center top of the cantle. Adult Western seats range, depending on style and model, from 14" to 18" lengths (increasing in one-half-inch incre- ments), though 15", 15½" and 16" are most common. Youth saddles usually run from 12" to 13". However, seat lengths can vary widely from saddle style to saddle style, and brand to brand — just because you ride in a 16" seat in your Brand A roper doesn't mean that you'll fit best in a 16" Brand B roper or a 16" Brand C reiner.

Saddle tree

The slope of the saddle seat is also important — your body will naturally slide to the lowest part of the seat, and where that is, in re- lation to the swells, cantle and stirrups, is critical to where — and how well — you balance in your saddle. In general, the steeper the front end of the saddle slopes up toward the horn, the more the sad- dle will hold you in position against the cantle; the lower, or flatter, the slope, the more room you'll have to move around in the saddle.

Also, the comfort of a certain seat shape will vary by rider gen- der. Women (whose seat bones are wider apart and whose thighs are usually rounder than men's) are generally most comfortable with a seat that's wider in the back, but with a narrow "twist" or "waist" between their upper thighs. A saddle with a wide waist will often push a woman's legs too too far forward and too far apart, making for an uncomfortable, unbalanced ride. Men, on the other hand, typi- cally prefer a somewhat flat seat with a wider twist, but not too wide at the back of the seat. A majority of cutting and roping saddles are made with wide twists, whereas most barrel-racing saddles are made more for women, with narrower twists.

The rigging

Although it has the least glamorous job — holding the saddle securely on the horse — the rigging is critical to your safety and your (and your horse's) performance. There are almost as many ways to tie your saddle onto your horse — and about as many opinions on which are best — as there are saddle styles. If you look in just about any catalog or tack store, though, two styles are clearly most popular — the double-ring (or double-dee) rigging and the in-skirt rigging.

The double-ring rigging consists of two rings (usually D-shaped) on each side of the saddle, one under the swells and one under the cantle, hung by sturdy leather straps directly onto the saddle tree, and connected to each other by another leather strap under the saddle seat. When used correctly with a rear cinch, the double-dee rigging is perhaps the most sturdy and stable way to cinch a saddle in place, which is why it's preferred by ropers. A dropped-dee rigging features a front ring placed lower on the horse, so it wraps the body even more securely.

In-skirt riggings, on the other hand, attach the rings to the saddle skirts instead of to the trees. Best used for easier-on-the-saddle disciplines (such as Western pleasure showing and trail riding), the in-skirt rigging reduces bulk under the rider's legs. It also allows for more freedom of movement for the rider's leg, so it's often found on barrel-racing saddles. However, because it snugly wraps the front

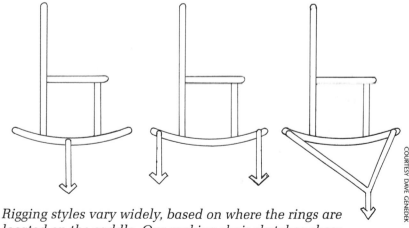

Rigging styles vary widely, based on where the rings are located on the saddle. Our rocking chair sketches show the concepts behind the (left to right) center fire, double-dee and flat-plate riggings.

COURTESY DAVE GENEDEK

skirt around the horse's shoulders, an in-skirt rigging may hinder optimum movement and performance. Also, most riders who use an in-skirt rigging do not use the back cinch.

A J-rig is a type of in-skirt rigging that further reduces bulk under the rider's leg by cutting out the skirt: When you cinch up, the latigo settles into the cut-out, instead of adding thickness on top of the skirt.

One of the best rigging styles (for evenly distributing pressure and for allowing freedom of movement) is the flat-plate rigging, which forms a triangle with the front and rear rings. Because cinching up a flat-plate rigging pulls on both the front and, to a degree, the rear of the saddle, a rear cinch is less necessary.

In addition to rigging styles, a saddle's specifications will include a rigging position. If the center of the D-ring is lined up with the center of the swell, that's known as full position. Full position, used in conjunction with a rear cinch, is most often found on roping saddles. Center-fire position, seldom used these days (except on some working-ranch saddles), is when the D-ring is hung directly under the center of the seat.

The rest of the positions — ⅝, ¾ and ⅞ — are proportional distances from center-fire to full. Many of the most popular saddle styles and models today are rigged at ⅞ position, although some saddle makers believe that ¾ position gives the horse more freedom of leg and shoulder movement.

Some in-skirt riggings feature three-way rigging plates, which allow you to move the latigo based on how the saddle fits on different horses. The front slot is used for a full position; the second one is ¾ position; and if you make a triangle between the two of them, that's ⅞ position.

Sport-specific saddles

Especially in saddle styles, form follows function. Today, there are saddles made specifically for certain disciplines, as well as "general-purpose" saddles. If you intend to seriously compete in a certain sport, a saddle specially designed with those challenges and demands in mind will serve you better than an all-purpose saddle, which is made more for the rider who likes to dabble casually in lots of different disciplines.

■ ***Cutting:*** *Designed with a relatively flat seat to give the rider plenty of room and freedom to move around in* *order to stay out of the horse's way as he follows the cow. Usually features a tall, slim horn for easy gripping and oxbow stirrups.*

■ ***Reining:*** *Shaped to hold the rider basically in one spot — against the back of the saddle — for stability during spins and sliding stops. As a result, the seat of a reining saddle is typically built up higher in front, as well as in the cantle.*

■ ***Roping:*** *Saddle must be extra sturdy and stable on the horse's back to withstand jarring jolts, so it almost always has traditional on-tree, double-ring rigging, used with both a front and back cinch. Usually features a "slick" fork, so the rope won't hang up, a reinforced horn and a low cantle, usually about only 2" to 3" high, for speedy dismounts. Stirrup treads are typically broader than most to support more of the rider's foot when standing to rope.*

■ ***Barrel racing and endurance riding:*** *Designed to be lightweight and less restrictive to the horse's movement, often with round or butterfly skirts. Usually sized down in the seat and twist to fit women.*

■ ***Pleasure saddles:*** *Designed primarily for the comfort of both rider and horse, these usually feature in-skirt riggings, a rather "deep" seat (built-up front and moderate-to-high cantle) and moderately broad bell-shaped stirrups.*

Keep in mind: *If you're planning to work young horses (who are likely to spook, buck, bolt or rear), you won't want to select a flat-seated saddle with a slick fork and low cantle — a wide-swell fork and moderate-to-high cantle will help keep you in your seat by giving your legs and seat something to brace against.*

Latigos and cinches

On both sides of the saddle, the latigos (sometimes, there's a shorter "billet" on the saddle's off side) attach the rigging rings to the cinch, which encircles the horse's belly. Because the latigo plays a key role in keeping your saddle (and you) on your horse, it should be made of high-quality material and should be inspected regularly for wear.

Western front cinches are made of many materials, including mohair, cotton, nylon and rayon. Mohair is soft and easy on the horse's skin, as is cotton, but cotton tends to rot and fray after heavy use. Synthetic materials, such as nylon and rayon, are strong, durable and easy to clean.

Rear cinches are most often made of leather. Used primarily on heavy-use saddles (i.e., roping) with double-dee riggings, the rear cinch holds down the back of the saddle. In many speed and agility disciplines, such as reining and barrel racing, riders often prefer no rear cinch, with the idea of reducing interference with the horse's hindquarters.

The skirts

Lined with fleece or wool, skirts (the large pieces of leather that extend in front, behind and below the saddle seat) help protect the horse's back by padding under the bars and rigging, and they somewhat help hold the saddle in place. Larger skirts add weight but provide more coverage (important if you're riding in rough countryside); smaller skirts are lightweight and give the horse more freedom to move but are less protective.

Styles include the traditional square skirts; round skirts, which are often found on Arabian saddles; and "butterfly" skirts, which are deep in front and high in the rear (shaped like a butterfly's wing), often preferred by barrel racers and endurance riders.

Stirrups and fenders

Western stirrups are available in many shapes, typically designed with a specific use in mind. Pleasure riding (trail and show) saddles usually have stirrups that are bell-bottomed styled, with a level, 2" to 2½" wide flat tread, which supports the ball of the rider's foot. Ropers, especially, want stirrups with even wider treads (such as

3") for support while standing. Cutters and working cowboys, on the other hand, often prefer a narrower, oxbow-shaped stirrup that's most comfortable when the rider's heel is pushed forward against the stirrup.

Many saddle buyers simply stick with the stirrup that comes with the saddle, without considering whether it's the right size for their feet. A stirrup that's too small can quickly become uncomfortable, whereas one that's too big or too small is a safety risk, allowing your foot to get stuck or slip all the way through and get "hung up." As a rule of thumb, look for about one finger's width of clearance between your foot and the edge of the stirrup.

A term you'll often hear in conjunction with stirrup leathers is "Blevins quick-change buckles." Offering ease of stirrup-length adjustment, the Blevins buckle is also less bulky under the rider's leg than the old-style roller buckles. ■PH■

Notes

18

Does Your Saddle Fit?

*You don't have to be an expert to tell
whether your saddle is potentially hurting your horse.
To find out, put your saddle to the "Fit-ness Test."*

When was the last time you walked into a tack shop where all the saddles were displayed upside down, boldly baring their underbellies? Truth be told, saddle-selling would certainly make more sense that way. After all, the side of the saddle that sits on the horse has far more impact on his performance than the side that we sit on. With a little savvy about saddle undersides, you can quickly pinpoint potential trouble spots and prevent your horse from being pinched, pounded or poked by a poorly fitting saddle.

Saddle essentials

The saddle's framework — its tree — is the single most important factor in saddle fit. No amount of fancy leatherwork will make a finished saddle fit your horse if the bare tree doesn't fit him to begin with. And although we can easily see the parts of the tree that affect how the saddle fits our seat, it's primarily the bars of the tree, hidden inside under leather and fleece, that affect how the saddle fits the horse.

Bars should be broad, smooth (not lumpy) and symmetrical (same shape, width and angle on both sides) because their job is to evenly distribute the rider's weight over the horse's back. Equally important, if the bars don't uniformly follow the contours and curves of

On a Western saddle without a pad, you want only two fingers clearance above the withers, and barely four fingers clearance with a pad. More than that, the saddle will be too narrow. This saddle is just borderline. Note that with an average-thickness pad, there's a generous four-finger-plus clearance. That means the saddle will ride high and the weight will not be distributed properly — resulting in a sore-backed horse.

your horse's back, the saddle can, at the least, hinder your horse and, at worst, seriously harm him.

The distance between the tops of the bars — the gullet channel that runs the length of the saddle — is also crucial. A properly fitted saddle actually rests on the horse's rib cage and supporting muscles. If the gullet is too narrow, the bars may painfully press on the edge of the spine, especially when the horse works in small circles. If the spread is too wide, the saddle may sit too low and may tend to roll.

ONE OF RIDERS' MOST COMMON
MISTAKES IS PUTTING THEIR SADDLES
TOO FAR FORWARD.

Saddle sizing and fit problems

Western saddles are generally sold in four widths — full Quarter Horse (designed for stocky, well-muscled horses with low withers), Thoroughbred or standard (for horses with high, narrow withers), semi-Quarter Horse (for horses built somewhere between full Quarter Horse and Thoroughbred) and Arabian (for a horse with low, wide withers and a short back). However, each horse has a uniquely shaped back, and not all horses conform to their breed's stereotypes, so you can't rely solely on guidelines.

Off-the-rack English saddles are traditionally available in three tree widths, appropriately classified as wide, medium and narrow. Unfortunately, however, those terms are not standardized across the industry, so a "wide" in one brand of saddle may be a "medium" in another brand. And, of course, sizing by tree width doesn't take into account the length of the saddle, so a saddle that fits the back breadth may still be too long, gouging into the withers and/or loins, whereas a saddle that's too short won't spread your weight over a large enough area.

By far, say many saddle fitters, the most common saddle-fit problem is "bridging." When a saddle makes a four-point contact on the horse's withers and loins, with no contact along the big muscles of the horse's back, the saddle is said to "bridge." This is most typically a problem with saddles that lack enough "rocker," or bow in the middle, to follow the natural dip in most horses' backs between the shoulders and the loins.

On the other hand, a saddle with too much rocker will seesaw with extreme pressure in the middle of the horse's back, teeter-tottering back and forth as he moves. This problem most often occurs in very flat-backed (or roach-backed) horses.

Finally, some saddles are simply off-balanced. On well-designed saddles, the center (and lowest part) of the seat is centered over the lowest part of the horse's back. On many saddles, the lowest part of the seat is too far back, which concentrates the rider's weight down on the horse's loins and impedes the power and action of his hindquarters.

Of course, an ill-fitting saddle is not the only cause of poor performance in the horse. Conformation weaknesses, harsh bits and unbalanced hooves can all cause back pain. Also, even if your saddle fits perfectly, you may inadvertently alter its pressure-bearing surfaces and cause saddle sores if you constantly stand in the stirrups, lean too far forward or back, or ride limp, slouched or off-centered.

Adding to the complexity of saddle fit is that horses don't stay the same from year to year, even season to season. The fit of your saddle may change over time as your horse matures, gains or loses weight, or progresses in training (which may affect muscle mass). So check your saddle regularly during the riding season to catch potential problems before they start.

Using pads to improve fit

Ideally, a properly fitting saddle needs nothing more than a thin pad or Navajo blanket as a dirt shield, moisture/heat wick and fashion statement (if you like a splash of color). Few horses, however, have perfectly shaped backs or perfectly fitting saddles, so in some cases, corrective padding can be helpful.

For instance, a horse whose back is asymmetrical (from injury, conformation or unbalanced conditioning) may need shims to shore up the gaps in saddle-bar contact. Or a horse who has lost weight over the riding season may need extra padding to help narrow a tree that has become a bit too wide. Or a horse whose back begins to dip as he ages may need padding under the center of his saddle to keep it from bridging.

Pads can't help a too-narrow saddle, however; instead, they usually make the situation worse, like adding an extra pair of socks under too-tight shoes. Also, keep in mind that the thicker your padding, the more likely your saddle is to roll or rock. Anytime you use shims or thick pads, make sure the saddle doesn't sit too high off the horse's back or tip backward or forward.

The saddle "fit-ness test"

Instead of going by sold-as sizes, you're more likely to get an accurate, comfortable fit by selecting a saddle the same way you'd buy a pair of shoes for yourself — by trying it on — and checking for the following criteria. More than likely, your saddle fits your horse well if it:

■ Clears the withers under the fork or pommel, while you're sitting in the saddle, by two to three fingers' width (however, too much clearance — more than three fingers — often indicates that the tree is too narrow).

■ Spans the spine down the length of the gullet (with an unobstructed channel about two or three inches wide).

■ Spreads your weight over broad, smooth bars or panels.

■ Maintains uniform contact along the contours of your horse's back.

■ Positions the lowest part of the saddle (which should be in the middle of the saddle) over the lowest part of your horse's back.

■ Allows for free shoulder movement (ideally, the saddle tree should sit a couple of finger widths behind the shoulder blade).

■ Is the proper length for your horse's back, neither too short (which would cause excessive pressure over too-small an area, particularly on top of his loins) nor too long (which would jab him in the hip bone).

■ Sits securely on your horse's back, with no tendency to rock or slide around, even while you mount and dismount.

Rigging — the way the saddle is "tied onto" your horse — is another key part of the puzzle. Faulty or ill-designed rigging can completely negate an otherwise ideal fit. (In the next chapter, we'll fully explain various saddle-rigging designs and their intricacies; but for now, there are a couple of key points you should consider when saddling up.)

When cinched up, the girth should settle in the hollow just in front of the horse's belly, without galling his elbows. Also, the girth should hang straight down from the tree. A girth that angles forward will exert too much pressure on the front of the saddle, instead of equally through the length of the saddle.

Even if your saddle passes the criteria above, a few additional "fit-ness exams" can help you confirm its fit before you mount and ride off.

■ First, with your cinched-up saddle, slip your hand under the front of the bars. Can you slide your hand in easily, or does it feel pinched or squeezed? If your hand is uncomfortable, your horse is, too.

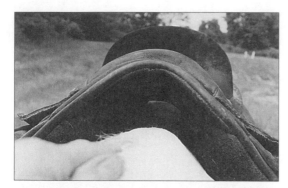

This saddle shows a nice, wide gullet, and the panels follow the contour of the horse, which is what you want.

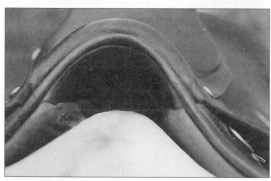

This gullet is too narrow. You can see it is also uneven; the right side of the saddle is higher than the left. It is not uncommon for used or even new saddles to be crooked.

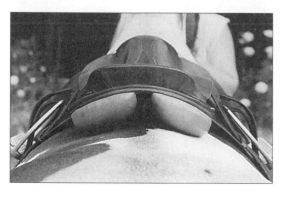

Looking at the same saddle from the back, you can see how its crookedness will put pressure on the right side of horse's back, in addition to pinching up in the withers area.

■ Ask a friend to extend your horse's front leg out front while you leave your hand under the front bar. Does the tree still clear the shoulder blade as it rotates back? If not, it will inhibit your horse's movement.

■ Run your hand under the back bars of the saddle. Are there gaps there, with very little pressure? If so, either the bars curve too far upward or the saddle is balanced too far to the front.

■ Finally, lift the flaps or fenders and run your hand up under the middle of the saddle. Is there a gap? If so, the saddle is "bridging" and will place undue pressure on the withers and loins.

■ Still not certain? Try the powder test. First, lightly dust the underside of your saddle with flour or baby powder. Next place the saddle on your horse's back, cinch it down lightly, then lift the saddle directly up off the horse's back (don't slide it as you lift, or you'll smear the results). The saddle's "footprint," left by the powder residue on your horse's back, will show you where the saddle is — and isn't — contacting your horse's back.

To account for changes in the shape of your "loaded" horse's back, you may also want to try the same test with your weight in the saddle, if you can mount and dismount without the saddle sliding. (Ask someone to boost you into the saddle, while you hold the mane for balance.)

Telltale signs of poor fit

Certainly, puffy swellings and raw sores are a clear signal that a saddle doesn't fit. However, tissue trauma can also occur out of sight, deep down in the muscles, which are more sensitive to pressure damage. You can be fairly certain that your saddle doesn't fit (and may be hurting your horse) if:

■ You're constantly readjusting the saddle's position while you ride.

■ It sinks down in front, with too little clearance under the fork or pommel, or rubs your horse's withers (the tree in front is too wide).

■ The fork or pommel is too high and the cantle too low (the tree is too narrow).

■ It often rolls to the side when you try to mount (too wide).

■ It constantly slides back while you ride (too narrow).

■ You're constantly having to pull your legs back to keep them under you, or you feel that you're often behind the horse's movement (a too-narrow tree may be tipping the saddle back or the stirrups may be hung too far forward, forcing your legs forward "onto the dashboard").

■ After a ride, your horse's hair is roughed-up around the saddle edges, indicating that the saddle slides around and rubs a lot.

■ The saddle leaves uneven sweat patterns on your horse's back after a ride (dry spots may indicate excessive pressure, or no pressure, in those areas).

■ Your horse's back develops white patches, where pressure points have damaged the hair follicles.

You should also consider the possibility that your saddle doesn't fit if your horse is free-moving and smooth-gaited on a lunge line but stiff, short-strided and choppy when carrying weight. Saddle discomfort may also be the reason he fidgets or rears during mounting, is sullen or ill-tempered under saddle, constantly wrings his tail, won't lower his head under saddle, resists transitions and lead changes, bucks after a jump, stiffens on tight turns, resents working up and down hills, travels with his head cocked off to one side, or resists collection or backing.

Put your saddle in the right spot

Experts agree: One of riders' most common mistakes is putting their saddles too far forward. If the front edge of your saddle hits your horse's shoulder blade as he moves, his stride will shorten, and the saddle will bruise and make his back sore. Also, a saddle placed too far forward can cause the seat to slope toward the back of the saddle, forcing your weight too far back and your legs too far forward, throwing you out of balance and often putting you "behind the movement."

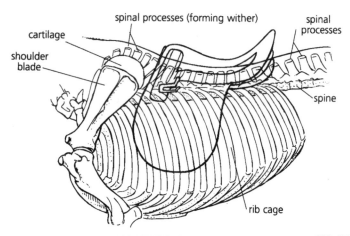

ART COURTESY OF TRAFALGAR SQUARE PUBLISHING 802-457-1911.
FROM *FOR THE GOOD OF THE HORSE* BY MARY WANLESS.

Before you girth up, run your hand firmly back along the shoulder blade until your fingertips "fall off the bone." Then, position your saddle so that the front edge of the saddle's tree is a couple of inches behind the shoulder blade (the skirts of a Western saddle, however, can lie over the top of the blade, as long as they don't gouge into it). This ensures that as your horse's front legs move forward (which tilts the shoulder blade back), his shoulders can move freely. Watch that the back of the skirt does not bump into the horse's hips.

While this is the ideal placement, unfortunately, many Western saddles are designed to rest on the horse's shoulders. With such a saddle, if you slide it back to a position that frees the shoulder, the seat's balance may change, tipping you forward, and the fork may no longer clear the withers. To avoid this problem, look for a saddle where the lowest part of the seat is at the midpoint (in the center) of the saddle, not back close to the cantle.

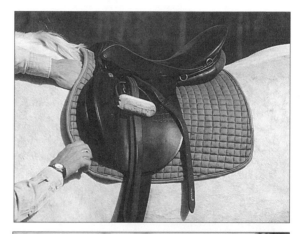

Check first under the front of the saddle to see that there's not too much pressure. Check the middle of the saddle to be sure it makes contact with the horse's back and doesn't "bridge," which will create excessive pressure by the horse's shoulders and under the cantle of the saddle.

If you're stuck with this kind of saddle, make sure you can easily slide your hand under the front skirts, between the saddle and the horse's shoulder blade, after you've cinched up the saddle. If you feel pressure there, your saddle will interfere with the free movement of your horse's front legs. In some cases, you may be able to add a bit of padding under the middle of your saddle to slightly raise the front of the bars off the shoulder. You'll then need to use your back cinch more snugly to keep the saddle from rocking back and forth. Keep in mind, however, this is a temporary "band-aid"; ideally, you should look for a new saddle that doesn't sit on your horse's shoulders.

"Fitness Test"

Take a moment, each time you ride, to run through this quick checklist.

Before you saddle up:
■ *Examine your saddle's underside for lumpiness, asymmetry and a gullet channel of at least two inches.*

After you girth up:
■ *Make sure the front bars aren't pinching your horse's shoulder blades (check both sides for shoulder clearance and excessive pressure).*
■ *Lift the fenders or stirrup flaps to feel under the saddle bars for even contact along the length of the horse's back.*

After you mount:
■ *Check for at least 1½" clearance under the fork or pommel.*
■ *Make sure the saddle neither rocks from front to back nor rolls from side to side.*

After you ride:
■ *Look for uneven sweat patterns and dry spots on the horse's back.*
■ *Re-examine the saddle underside for uneven wear patterns.* PH

19

Finding The Right Fit

From high-touch to high-tech,
several techniques and technologies can help
you find a saddle that comfortably fits your horse.

L ast chapter, along with a look at the basic concepts of saddle fit, we outlined a simple "fit-ness test" to help you judge whether your own saddle truly fits your horse (or potentially causes him "fits"). Well, how did your saddle do? If you're like some horseowners, you may have discovered that your horse's back is getting pinched or poked every time you cinch him up (and we all know that a horse who hurts is unlikely to be a perfect horse, in either performance or attitude). Or you may have found that although your saddle fits reasonably well in most places, it needs some minor adjustments here or there. So now what?

Actually, you have several options, depending on the extent of the problem. We'll walk you through a logical plan of action for finding the right fit for your horse.

A quick fit review

Fit-wise, the most important part of the saddle is the tree. As the saddle's framework, hidden under layers of leather and fleece, the tree transfers the rider's weight onto the horse's back. How well the tree matches the curves and angles of the horse's back determines how evenly the rider's weight is distributed onto the horse. If the tree is too narrow, too wide, too long or too short, or if there's too little curve in the middle (or too much), the saddle can put intense

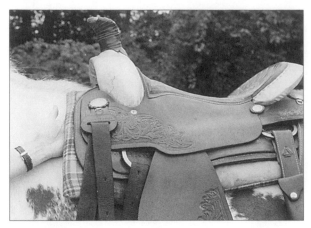

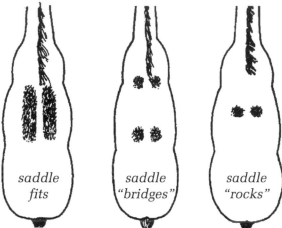

saddle
fits

saddle
"bridges"

saddle
"rocks"

Ideally, the rider's weight should be distributed along the muscles of the horse's back. If the saddle "bridges," there will be four pressure points. If the saddle "rocks," it will create two pressure points. To check for pinching at the withers, put your fingers under the front of the saddle, and with a rider on board, walk along with the horse.

pressure in some areas, causing tissue damage and muscle soreness. Looking only at a saddle's topside, however, will seldom tell you if it fits; you must run your hand along the underside, between the horse and saddle (after it's cinched up), to detect some of the most significant problems.

Can you make it fit?

The first question you should always consider is whether your current saddle is salvageable. In many cases, a not-quite-right fit can be fixed for far less than the price of a new saddle. A saddler may be able to modify your current saddle. Or, sometimes, creative shimming or padding can help.

Let's say, for instance, you've discovered that your saddle "bridges" (sits only on your horse's shoulders and loins, with no contact in the middle of his back), which saddle experts agree is the No. 1 problem with Western saddles. If the bridging isn't too extreme, a competent saddler may be able to add a few layers of leather to the middle underside of your saddle tree (up under the fleece); with a bit more "rocker," your saddle may follow the contours of your horse's back better.

If you don't have a good saddler nearby, or if you use the same saddle for different horses (and, so, don't want a permanent change to your saddle), you may be able to use extra padding, or temporary shims, under the middle of the saddle. As master saddler Dave Genadek advises, the rule of thumb is to "pad away from pressure." If your saddle bridges, don't add pads under the pressure spots, which only worsens the problem (like pulling on an extra pair of socks when your shoes are already too tight). Instead, add shims where there are gaps in contact, to equalize the pressure.

Another common problem, for both Western and English saddles, is too much width in the front part of the tree, particularly for Thoroughbred-type horses with narrow withers. One solution is to use just enough extra padding under the front part of the bars to raise the front of the saddle to the correct position; however, you must then make sure that you haven't shifted too much pressure to the back of the saddle or inadvertently caused the saddle to bridge in the middle. And, any time you use shims or extra pads, the edges should be beveled and smooth to avoid creating hard, uncomfortable ridges under the saddle.

With English saddles, the panels can become lumpy or uneven. If so, your wool-stuffed saddle may simply need to be restuffed, or "reflocked."

A saddler may also be able to reposition your saddle's rigging, if need be, or replace worn fleece under a Western saddle. Unfortunately, some saddles simply can't be "fixed" to fit certain horses. If your saddle is too long, or your tree too narrow, or the balance way off center, you may have to buy another saddle.

In a tack store stuffed with saddles — new and used, in all styles, shapes and sizes — finding one that fits would seem fairly easy. Experts say, however, that the odds of walking out with a well-fitting saddle on the first try or two are slim. Even an experienced saddler would be hard-pressed to eyeball the underside of a saddle and know for certain that it would fit a particular horse. But don't despair, saddle-fit specialists have devised a few clever ways around the problem.

Withers tracings

To take your own withers tracings, you'll need a wire or flexible curve about 24" long (flexible curves are available at some art shops or office-supply stores for around $10). You'll also need a few large pieces of cardboard (manila file folders will do), a piece of chalk, a pencil, a ruler and a pair of scissors.

For an English saddle, you'll take three tracings — one about ½" behind the horse's shoulder blade, one at the lowest part of his back, and one where the cantle would sit. For a Western saddle, you may also need a tracing across the midpoint of the withers, since many Western saddles are designed to sit on top of the horse's shoulders, over the withers.

To start your tracings, make sure your horse is standing up "square" (don't let him slump or lean off to one side), with his head in a natural position (where he'd correctly carry it, while under saddle). Then, drape the flexible curve across his back in one of the tracings positions listed above. Gently press and mold both sides of the curve to evenly contact the horse's body. Then, before you remove the curve, use a piece of chalk to mark on the horse where you've taken the tracing. Finally, lift the flexible curve from the horse's back, put it down flat on a piece of cardboard and trace the inner edge of the curve onto the cardboard.

Under each tracing, remember to write down the tracing position (withers, behind the shoulder, mid-point or cantle), as well as which side was the horse's right side, and which was his left. Also, measure — and make a note on each template — how far the tracing was taken from adjacent tracings (so you'll know how to position your templates under the saddle).

Then, cut along each tracing line and discard the top parts. What's left are templates of your horse's back that you can take to the tack shop and hold under each corresponding part of the saddle to check for fit.

Saddle-fit expert Jan Jacobson also recommends taking a "spinal curvature" tracing — by molding the flexible curve down the length of the horse's back, from withers to loins — to make sure the saddle will have the right "rocker" in the middle, to follow any dip in the horse's back.

If you have difficulty finding a flexible curve, **Performance Saddlery** sells a "Horse Fit Kit," complete with flexible curve and detailed instructions, as well as directions for ordering a custom-fit English saddle. The Horse Fit Kits sells for $29.99 separately, or for just $10 when ordered with saddle-maker Jan Jacobson's $49.99 video set for fitting English saddles.

Above, mark three locations where you'll be measuring. Then measure (level) the distance between points so you can place the templates in the correct position inside your saddle.

Then measure following the spine.

The first measurement ("W") is taken on the withers. You can see how difficult it would be to place the flexible rule in the same place twice if you didn't mark the horse.

The second measurement ("A") is taken behind the horse's shoulder blade. "B" and "C" are taken farther back. The "W" or withers measurement, that Jan took in the photo at the top of this page, is under her watchband. You can see the importance of putting markings on the horse.

Using our withers-tracing templates, we put "A" template in the correct position under our Western saddle. It shows us that this saddle would be too small in the gullet for our horse ("A" is tight), and that there's a gap on one side. So, the rider's weight wouldn't be distributed correctly. The skirts of the saddle do not carry any weight; only the tree does, which extends only about 4" down the side — almost to "L," for instance.

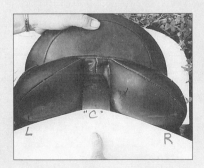
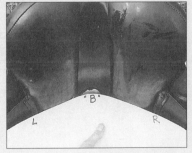

On this saddle, the weight-bearing surface is adequate, but it could be better. The panels of the saddle are too hard to spread contact with the horse's back out very far. You can see the same thing by looking at "B" under the saddle.

Your horse's shape

Old-timers once relied on bending a coat hanger over the horse's withers. They could then take a shaped replica to the tack shop or saddle-maker and hold it up under each saddle to check for fit. Withers tracings are more refined but not the only method of determining your horse's shape.

Veterinarian and saddle-fit expert Joyce Harman, of Harmany Equine Clinic, suggests that making a plaster mold of your horse's back is another useful technique for checking saddle fit. Although making a plaster mold is a bit more messy and time-consuming than withers tracings, the result can be more accurate, especially in replicating the curves of the horse's back in relation to each other. This may not be the most realistic solution for most people, however.

While withers tracings and plaster molds will often "put you in the right ballpark," some tack stores and saddlers offer more precise methods of measuring for fit.

Looking much like a long metal spider with eight to 10 legs or "wings" (eight for English, 10 for Western), the Saddletech Gauge measures the angles of the horse's withers, shoulders, back and loins in exact numerical calibrations. After each wing is carefully adjusted to fit the horse's back, the Saddletech Gauge can then be held up under the saddle to see exactly where the saddle does and doesn't conform to the horse's curvature.

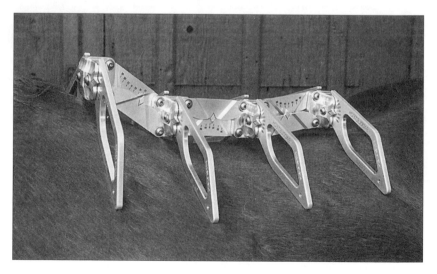

The Saddletech Gauge measures the back at fixed intervals.

One of the gauge's biggest benefits is that a horseowner can call in his horse's measurements to any tack shop with a Saddletech Gauge, and the saddler can adjust his own gauge to replicate the shape of the horse's back, right there in his shop, and hold it under his saddles, looking for one that fits.

Purchasing a Saddletech Gauge ($2,250 for 10-wing or $1,850 for 8-wing) is prohibitive for most horse owners. However, Saddletech maintains a nationwide network of tack shops, saddle-makers and veterinarians who offer Saddletech Gauge services. Some shops may offer the service at no charge; other professionals, such as veterinarians, will typically charge a fee (our informal poll indicated that standard fees can run from about $25 for a simple fit check to about $150 or more for a full session with several fittings).

You can also rent a gauge yourself, if you don't live near a gauge-owner or if you have several horses to measure. If you do decide to rent a gauge, be sure to follow the instructions carefully. Some of our saddle-fit consultants familiar with the gauge caution that truly accurate measurements can be tricky without patience and practice, especially if the horse doesn't stand quietly or exactly square, or if he holds his head incorrectly.

Pin-and-dowel devices, such as the Lauriche Back Graph and the Ultimate Saddle Checking System, allow you to "map" the horse's back.

ART COURTESY OF TRAFALGAR SQUARE PUBLISHING 802-457-1911. FROM *FOR THE GOOD OF THE HORSE* BY MARY WANLESS.

Of course, not all tack shops and saddle-makers use the Saddletech Gauge. Custom saddle-maker Rick Ricotti, for instance, shuns formal measurements and simply uses his own expertise and an extensive selection of bare trees to find the right fit.

Dr. Joyce Harman and Schleese Saddlery Service, on the other hand, use two different board-and-dowel systems (the Lauriche Back Graph and the Ultimate Saddle Checking System, respectively). By dropping more than 100 adjustable dowels or pegs down through a board framework, both systems can produce a three-dimensional form-likeness of the horse. Used extensively in Europe and England, the dowel system allows tree-makers and saddle-fitters to replicate the curves and hollows of the horse's back for a closer fit.

Saddle shopping

■ *Always ask about return policies before you buy or order a saddle. It's nearly impossible to know if a saddle will fit without trying it on the horse, even with the best gauges and measurement systems. Most reputable tack shops and mail-order companies will allow a trial-period.*

■ *Even if you find a particular saddle that fits your horse, keep in mind that another saddle in the same model and size may not fit, should you choose to look for a lower price elsewhere. Several factors affect how individual saddles fit, and not all trees are as uniformly made and shaped as you may think.*

■ *When you take a saddle home to "try it out," take special care to keep it from getting dirty or scratched. Trying to return a noticeably worn saddle (if you find it doesn't fit) will be much more difficult than taking it back in its original condition.*

The "rounding up" debate

As we talked with veterinarians and other experts on various saddle-fit issues, one particularly interesting topic of debate emerged. Many top horsemen assert that when a horse is properly collected and his hindquarters are "engaged," his back lifts slightly under the rider and "rounds up" into the saddle. So, in theory, a saddle that fits the horse while standing still could end up slightly rocking (putting more pressure in the middle) when he moves. This belief has encouraged some saddle-makers to fit saddles to slightly bridge the standing horse, in order to give him room to "round up" into the saddle as he moves.

Other horsemen say that horses do not, and cannot, lift their backs under the weight of a rider and that, at best, they simply brace themselves and hold their backs level. In fact, a couple of our consultants advise riders to fit their saddles to slightly rock on their unmounted horse to accommodate for the inevitable sag in his back when the rider gets on.

Interestingly, one of the three people we spoke with who've actually used computer-scanning systems to test the "rounding up" theory has scans that confirm some horses do round up (by virtue of increased pressure in the middle of the saddle when they move in a collected manner). The other two say they have scans to refute it (that if a saddle bridges the unmounted, unmoving horse, it will still bridge the mounted horse in motion).

So, how's a conscientious rider to fit his horse? By and large, the experts agree, if the horse is going to sag or raise his back at all, the difference will most likely be subtle. And, a horse's back is never static — it's in a constant state of flux, moving up, down and sideways during each and every ride. With that in mind (knowing you'll never find a saddle that perfectly fits your horse with every stride he takes), your best bet is to fit your horse as well as you can while he's standing still, unmounted, in a neutral position, as we outlined in last chapter's "Fit-ness Test."

The bottom line

When you consider all the factors that affect the saddle-fit equation, there's clearly no single formula or measurement system for finding a perfect fit. And how far you need to go to assure a good fit depends largely on your personal needs. If you're on a limited budget, looking for a mosey-around-the-farm saddle that's an acceptably comfortable fit, for instance, you needn't be as nit-picky as a serious high-level competitor, willing to spend what it takes to find a high-performance saddle that hugs your horse like his own hair coat.

And, as several of our saddle-fit consultants emphasized, the final judge — and the most important expert — is your horse. It doesn't matter what any saddle-seller says or what any measurement system indicates, if your horse isn't happy or comfortable under a certain saddle, don't buy it. ▣

Notes

Contacts

Advance Barn Construction
978-521-1171

Amoco Fabrics and Fibers Co.
800-445-7732/770-944-4568

Barns USA
800-881-0062/352-544-2746

Broadleaf P4
Broadleaf Industries, Inc.
800-628-7374/949-631-9266
www.broadleafp4.com

Brown Sprinkler Corporation
800-962-6274/317-889-4225
www.brownsprinkler.com

Cannon Ball • HNP
800-766-2825/608-365-2161
www.cnbhnp.com

CMW, Inc.
800-494-6623/606-254-6623
www.cmwequine.com

Country Manufacturing
740-694-9926
www.countrymfg.com

Cover-All Shelter
800-268-3768
www.coverall.net

Draw-Tite, Inc.
800-527-1740/518-561-4182
www.drawtite.com

Easy Rider (Busting Dust)
STS Products
800-845-9558/405-377-7333

Equiground and Ring Leveller
Equi-Master (USA) Inc.
800-544-5819/502-743-9158
www.eliteep.com

Equine Research Centre
519-837-0061
www.erc.on.ca

Fibar, Inc.
800-342-2721/914-273-8770
www.fibar.com

Fire-retardant-treated Wood
Hoover Treated Wood Company
877-722-6290/706-595-5058
www.frtw.com

Flame Control Coatings, Inc.
716-282-1399
www.flamecontrol.com

Footings Unlimited
Interland Group Inc.
800-972-7251

Fuerst Brothers
800-435-9630/217-784-5747
www.fuerst-bros.com

Gage-Babcock & Associates
914-273-2630
www.gbany1@aol.com

Dave Genadek
About the Horse, Inc.
800-449-7409/507-498-3668
www.aboutthehorse.com

Geosynthetics
ACF West, Inc.
800-878-5115/503-771-5115

Stan Gralla Architects
405-527-7000
www.telepath.com/gralla

Joyce Harman, DVM,
Harmany Equine Clinic
540-675-1855

Hayward Designs
513-681-5374
www.horsenet.com/hayward

Heartlight Enterprises
530-477-7050
www.heartlightenterprises.com

High Performance Arena Footing
Perma-Flex Inc.
800-993-9411/609-845-2875
www.perma-turf.com

Jan Jacobson
Performance Saddlery
800-258-0006/607-277-3541
www.saddlefit.com

KACE International
888-827-7789
www.kaceintl.com

Kaiser Construction Co., Inc.
610-385-4990
www.kaisereques.com

Lucas Equine Equipment, Inc.
606-234-6920

Maxi-flow Dry Hydrants
Red Head Brass, Inc.
800-321-3501/330-567-2903
www.readheadbrass.com

Ray Miller/Equiscan
800-354-8512

Millcreek
800-311-1323/717-355-2446

Morton Buildings, Inc.
800-447-7436/309-263-7474
www.mortonbuildings.com

National Equine Safety Assn.
800-643-3760

Plyco Corporation
800-558-5895/920-876-3611

Reese (hitches)
800-326-1090/219-264-7564
www.reeseprod.com

Rick Ricotti, Ricotti Saddle Co.
800-742-6884/209-759-3550

Kerry Ridgeway, DVM/Equisport
Center for Therapeutic Options
707-935-1825

Robert Ferrand, Saddletech
877-723-3538/650-343-9976
www.saddletech.com

Jochen Schleese
Schleese Saddlery Service
800-225-2242/905-898-8335
www.schleese.com

Shelton Industries
800-243-2421/513-734-2900
www.sheltonindustries.com

Soil Moist, JRM Chemical, Inc.
800-962-4010/216-475-8488
www.soilmoist.com

**Stock Safe Automatic Fire
Suppression Systems**
Hampshire Development
800-551-1988/603-642-9998

U-Haul
800-789-3638
www.uhaul.com

United Lightning Protection Assn.
800-668-8572/407-827-6153
www.ulpa.org

US Steel Buildings
800-222-6335/828-264-6198
www.ussteelbuildings.com

Valley Industries (hitches)
800-344-3112/209-368-8881
www.valleyindustries.com

Velux-America Inc.
800-888-3589/864-941-5360
www.VELUX.com

Madelon Wallace
800-442-4749/828-894-8220
wwe@teleplex.net

Walters Buildings
800-558-7800/414-629-5521
www.waltersbuildings.com

Wick Buildings
800-356-9682/608-795-2294
www.wickbuildings.com

■ ■ ■

Index

■ ■ ■

For information regarding *John Lyons' Perfect Horse*,
the monthly magazine, or other books in the John Lyons Perfect
Horse Library, see our web site www.perfecthorse.com
or call the publisher, Belvoir Publications, Inc. at 800-424-7887.

EXECUTIVE EDITOR: MAUREEN GALLATIN

ASSISTANT EDITORS: CINDY FOLEY AND LIZ NUTTER

CONTRIBUTING WRITERS: LEE FOLEY, ELEANOR KELLON VMD, LIZ NUTTER, L.A. POMEROY,
SUE STUSKA ED.D., KAY WHITTINGTON

BOOK DESIGN AND LAYOUT: SUSAN R. TOMKIN

PHOTO CREDITS: LEE FOLEY, MAUREEN GALLATIN, AMBER HEINTZBERGER, CHARLES HILTON,
JAN JACOBSON, ISABEL KUREK, SUE STUSKA, DONNA DIXON WOODALL